Flying With Wings

A True Story of an
Alaska Aircraft Accident

Susan Stark Christianson

Prologue and Epilogue by
Bob Jacobsen

Mason Works Press

Published by **Mason Works Press,** 6525 Gunpark Drive, #370-426, Boulder, Colorado, 80301.

www.FlyingWithWings.com

Cover photo of the Juneau Icefield taken by Mark Kelley shows the Devils Paw, the boarder between Canada and Alaska, in the background. Copyright © 1994, **Mark Kelley Photography**, Juneau, Alaska.

Cover design by **Matt Knutson**, Juneau, Alaska.

Interior graphic "Wings of Alaska" reprinted with permission by artist **Laurie Ferguson Craig**, Juneau, Alaska

ISBN: 978-0-578-27780-6 (Softcover)
ISBN: 979-8-218-26678-3 (Hard bound)
First Edition
Library of Congress Control Number: Pending

Printed in Canada Friesens Corporation

Dedicated to Karen Jacobsen, Timothy Miller
and the victims and survivors
of Wings of Alaska's 1994 accident.

Contents

"Wings of Alaska" by Laurie Ferguson Craig

"Wings of Alaska" is a hand-pulled, hand-colored etching featuring 50 Alaska birds in a circular pattern. The design of the print is indicative of a Tibetan mandala, a circular meditative symbol symmetrically balanced with a center and the cardinal points of north, south, east and west. Frequently, the complex patterns of mandalas show squares inside of concentric circles and represent the totality of the universe and its wholeness. In creating this piece, Juneau, Alaska artist Laurie Ferguson Craig combined the sense of balance and harmony seen in the natural environment with rich symbolism and a touch of Escher puzzle fitting in the arrangement of the birds. "It was a delight to see these beautiful creatures, who symbolize strength and grace, delicacy and power come together and fit so perfectly without being forced," Craig said. The etching was dedicated to the memory of Drew Haag, an Alaska Airlines Captain and co-founder of Wings of Alaska. "Drew was a friend who challenged all of us to spread our wings and fly," Craig said.

"When a story is told
it is not forgotten.
It becomes something else:
a memory of who we were;
a hope of what we can become."
-From Sarah's Key

Prologue

"Every person,
all the events of your life
are there because you have
drawn them there.
What you choose
to do with them
is up to you."
-Richard Bach
From the 1977 book "Illusions."

Flying With Wings is a true story about an Alaska aircraft accident written from the perspective of an omniscient narrator. The conversations, feelings and experiences in it, however, are based on a terrible tragedy that my company, Wings of Alaska, was responsible for in 1994. This is a very difficult book to read, especially for those who were involved.

As the President of Wings of Alaska, this is, in part, my story. It is also much more. For me, the purpose in agreeing to share these tragic details is simple: I hope to positively impact the far-too-many senseless aviation accidents still happening throughout Alaska and across the country. My friend and author, Susan Stark Christianson, witnessed many of these events and was motivated to tell the story for both aviation safety and another reason. She was inspired by the strength of survivors and their example of healing in the face of great loss and suffering. She hopes their story will help those going through their own difficulties and healing.

Over many months and years, Susan helped me sift through boxes of files pertaining to the accident; details saved for 30 years. I saved newspaper clippings, depositions, sworn affidavits, enforcement actions, faxes, and copies of all the legal bills. I saved every card sent by those who reached out in sympathy, kindness and support. Throughout the years I moved the boxes from the original Wings of Alaska hangar, to a new company hangar we built in 1997, to my personal office when we sold Wings of Alaska to an Oregon-based company in 2008.

While some artistic license has been taken and a few names have been changed, what you will read here stays true to what was shared by those who lived the actual events, the aftermath of the crash and the years of recovery. We spent years piecing together the perspectives and experiences of those involved. Together and alone, we talked with, interviewed and videotaped almost everyone involved - from accident survivors to family members of victims, from the rescue pilots and aircraft recovery team to the Federal Aviation Administration's lead attorney. Susan used the original faxes, depositions, enforcement proceeding transcripts, privileged legal communications, police reports, letters, affidavits, survivor statements, interviews and more to recreate the conversations and events shared in this book. Please check out the list of acknowledgements at the end for names of those interviewed or involved in our accident and its aftermath.

This story has many heroes. I trust that as you read *Flying With Wings*, you will be touched by the heartfelt dedication of the Wings of Alaska employees and their families, the community of Juneau, and by the inspirational lives of the survivors and the loved ones of those lost. The heroism survivors displayed in their journeys to healing and the examples they set for all of us in overcoming grief, trauma and tragedy continue to inspire.

It is my sincere hope that the mistakes we made as a company and the lessons we learned will benefit others in business, other private and commercial pilots and our friends in the Alaska aviation community. If we can help prevent one accident, then the telling of our story will have been worthwhile.

- Bob Jacobsen

Chapter One

A Barbecue 20 Years in the Making

The coals were hot and the sweet aroma of fresh-grilled Alaska salmon filled the air. King Crab dip from the popular local Juneau market Jerry's Meats and Seafoods, a garden-fresh vegetable tray and a variety of artfully prepared appetizers covered most every inch of the kitchen island. Wine glasses filled with chardonnay from a favorite Walla Walla, Washington winery stood next to bottles of Juneau-made Alaskan Amber and Icy Bay IPA.

It was a rare, sunny blue-sky Juneau day. From the street level on Gold Belt Avenue, looking up at the people standing on Bob and Darlene Jacobsen's front deck, the gathering appeared like any ordinary group of friends at an early summer barbecue; old friends sipping wine as they waited to eat, enjoying the sunlight reflecting off the water in Gastineau Channel and the majestic views of the snow-capped Mt. Juneau, Mt. Roberts and the Douglas Island peaks.

Darlene, a petite woman with glasses and long, silver-gray hair tied into a low ponytail, moved comfortably around her kitchen with quiet grace, filling glasses with the ease of an experienced entertainer and making sure the food trays all remained full.

The anticipation in the room grew as each new arrival walked through the door.

Rusty Shaub, the quiet, serious pilot and former Wings of Alaska Director of Operations and his wife Thyes were there. Michelle Ward, an Alaska Airlines flight attendant and one-half of the couple that own the historic Taku Glacier Lodge, traded small talk with Princess Cruise Line's manager Kirby Day. The always-effervescent Karen Jacobsen, Bob's sister and a Wings of Alaska owner, welcomed each new guest with a warm smile and friendly hugs. Everyone, from a former Wings of Alaska Director of Maintenance, to flight dispatchers, to past and current company pilots, had changed their plans on short notice in order to be at the Jacobsens barbecue that night, despite any personal apprehension they may have harbored. They came out of respect for the evening's guest-of-honor and because Bob Jacobsen invited them. They had no way of knowing just how much the experience they all shared exactly 20 years before still affected each of them.

***

Bob Jacobsen had received a phone call just days before. He left home early to work on his Cessna 180 at the family's private hangar located on Juneau's International Airport but remembered he needed to first stop by the Wings of Alaska hangar. He often stopped in to check on the new owners of the regional commuter airline that he and his best friend Drew Haag, with the help and mentorship of Mike Fenster, had started in 1982 with just two airplanes. Bob had presided over the business for 25 years before selling it. The company's new owners still leased airplanes from him and he had a financial interest in the business' success.

"Good morning Bob," said Scott Rinkenberger, the airline's new Southeast Alaska manager, as Bob approached the front door of the hangar and office building he and his sister had had built 17 years earlier.

"Someone here took a message from a guy last night who called looking for you. Did you get it yet?"

"No," Bob replied, wondering who would still be calling him at the Wings of Alaska offices. Everyone that he knew was aware he sold the Wings commuter airline business and had created a new company with former employees to grow the cruise-tour business to Taku Glacier Lodge. He couldn't imagine why anyone would still call for him at the Wings of Alaska offices.

"Someone called about an anniversary or something. I was planning to call you today to let you know. If you can wait a minute, I'll go upstairs to your old office and find the message."

Bob's heart skipped a beat and he had to remind himself to breathe.

He had a sinking feeling that the person in question might be one of the survivors of a Wings of Alaska plane that crashed into the inlet of Taku River on June 22, 1994, killing seven people, including two children. Hardly a day had gone by in those 20 years that

Bob hadn't looked at his own two handsome, healthy sons, Nathaniel and Christian, and thought about the two children whose lives were lost on his company's plane. He knew it wasn't entirely true, but Bob still blamed himself for the accident. As he felt the warm June breeze on his face, Bob stood silently dreading what might await him.

"Do you have any idea where the person calling was from?" he asked when Scott returned, trying to push down the emotions that seemed to well up to the surface too often these days. "Might Guatemala have been mentioned?" Bob asked.

"Yes, I think he said something about Guatemala," said Scott, confirming the source of Bob's growing anxiety.

Bob carefully folded the pink message slip Scott handed him and put it in the pocket of his black and blue-checkered fleece jacket. Still working to keep his mind and emotions under control, he finished his business and headed back to the old blue GMC truck parked in the hangar lot.

In all his years in business, Bob rarely showed his emotions. These days, however, he was having such a hard time keeping up his professional, cool and in-control façade.

A handsome man, with deep blue eyes and prematurely gray hair, Bob was well known and respected in the Juneau community where he was born and raised. As he drove the nine miles back from the airport to his house overlooking Alaska's capital, Bob did his best not to think about the events that surrounded the only fatal accident his company ever had. His hands were sweaty on the steering wheel.

Once back inside, Bob grabbed water from the kitchen and headed upstairs to his home office. Slowly he took the message paper from his jacket pocket, carefully unfolded it, and dialed the New York number.

"Hi. This is Bob Jacobsen from Juneau, Alaska." He looked down at the message again. "I'm returning David Elron's call," he said to the male voice that had answered the call.

"Well hello, Bob. This is David. I'm a good friend and counselor for Rosa Maria Gomar de Vides and I was actually calling on her behalf. Thank you so much for getting back to me."

"I have to say I was surprised to see your message," Bob said. "We actually sold Wings of Alaska six years ago and I just happened to stop by the office this morning to check in." The two men traded small talk about Alaska for a while before David shared the reason for his call.

"Well, I was reaching out because Rosa asked me for help getting in touch with someone at Wings of Alaska. She's thinking about coming to Juneau in two days for the anniversary of her mother and her children's deaths. I was wondering if there was anyone at Wings that might be available to help her out during her visit?"

Bob took another deep breath and exhaled slowly. "Of course," he said, taking a sip of water. "I was the President of Wings of Alaska at the time of the accident and would do anything I can to help Rosa, anything at all. I do understand if she doesn't want to see me..." His voice trailed off.

"Well, she hasn't decided for sure if she wants to come, but if you have some time this afternoon, I would appreciate if I could schedule a joint call between the three of us to talk about it more," David said. "She's thinking of coming with her cousin Gonzalo and her three teenage children. I trust that you know that this journey back to Juneau 20 years after the accident is very important to Rosa, and on a certain level, frightening. As her friend and counselor, however, I've been encouraging Rosa to make the trip."

Every year on the anniversary of the accident Rosa had asked herself if she was ready to go back to Juneau. Every year before this one the answer was always clearly "No." But this year when she prayed and meditated, things felt different. "It all looked sunny and translucent," Rosa had told her healer and mentor. She had tried making summer plans for Lucia, Ana and Jesus, but the plans kept falling through and Rosa began to think this might be the year she was supposed to go.

Bob looked down at his cell phone. The date was June 20, 2014. It was almost 20 years to the day from the date of the accident that still haunted his dreams.

"Of course," he said. "I'm available any time and will do anything to help facilitate her visit here."

"How about we set up a call at 2 p.m. Alaska time?" David asked. "I'll call Rosa Maria and arrange it with her. Just knowing that you will be there and are willing to offer your help leaves me with peace and a mountain of gratitude. I look forward to the three of us talking soon."

Area Map
Juneau-Taku Inlet

Chapter Two

June 22, 1994 - A Typical Day for Flying

George Coulter kissed his wife Karen goodbye then poured one last, strong cup of coffee into his thermos. Balancing the thermos and his keys in one hand while he opened the front door, George stopped for a moment to listen to the weather forecast on the KINY radio morning news.

"Typical Juneau-weather day," he thought. "High overcast. Light morning fog. We'll fly today."

George, a stocky man in his early 50s, loved his job as a pilot for Wings of Alaska. He'd been flying small planes in Alaska for more than 12 years, yet he still showed excitement sharing the thrill of flying in a deHavilland Otter float plane with the thousands of visitors who came to Alaska's capital city every year. He loved seeing the beauty of Southeast Alaska through their eyes and never tired of telling visitors facts about the land, glaciers and waterways as he helped them climb aboard a floatplane for their Wings of Alaska - Taku Glacier Lodge adventure. Most of the visitors had never experienced flying on a floatplane before, let alone flying above a glacier or through the Alaskan wilderness.

George considered himself privileged to have a job at Wings, where every day he could admire the beauty of the granite peaks that emerge from the spectacular ice fields. Flying above the Norris, Taku, Hole-in-the-Wall and East and West Twin glaciers was still awe-inspiring, even though he had done it hundreds of times. It wasn't unusual for him to see a black bear, moose, eagles and other wildlife from his private perch in the plane's cockpit. He loved the feeling of descending over Twin Glacier Lake, over the birch trees, spruce, alders and cottonwoods along Sockeye Flats. He loved the rustic beauty of 80-year-old Taku Glacier Lodge standing alone on top of its grassy knoll.

George had aspired to be a pilot since he was a small boy and he was a good pilot. It still irked him, though, that Bob Jacobsen - the kid George taught to fly when he was a flight instructor in Oregon - had recently demoted him from Chief Pilot to regular line pilot at the company. "I can't believe Bob thinks Rusty Shaub or Mike Stedman can do a better job managing things than I can. It's all that darn paperwork, I suck at ..." His thoughts trailed off as he focused on putting the key into his truck's ignition.

"It's going to be a long day," he thought, pulling out of his driveway. "I've got to remember to stop and pick up a nice gift for Karen for our wedding anniversary tomorrow. Where the heck did 23 years go?"

***

Sitting in his office atop the Wings of Alaska hangar, Bob Jacobsen was surrounded by images of flight. The paintings surrounding his desk by renowned Alaskan artists Herb Bonnet, Byron Birdsall and John Fehringer captured images of float planes soaring high above Alaska's majestic peaks, inland waterways and glacial ice. The artists shared the wall space with Jacobsen family photos and historic pictures of Juneau's airport. A Fred Machetanz painting of a weathered, old Alaskan sourdough hung directly behind his chair. It was as if the rough-and-rowdy spirits of the pioneers who built Alaska watched over him as he worked.

A wooden sign from an old airline, Fox Air Service, sat on the floor juxtaposed with a Southeast Skyways flight bag, Schwinn bicycle, books and boxes of financial records. Piles of papers and trade magazines lay neatly on the desk. A model of Alaska Airlines 737-200QC, N742AS, referred to in aviation circles as "FLUF," teetered precariously atop a bookcase, as if it too was ready for takeoff.

Under Bob's watchful eye, Wings of Alaska – the business he and his best friend Drew Haag had started in 1982 with just two airplanes - had become a successful and respected commuter air carrier in the state. The business provided scheduled passenger, freight and mail service throughout Northern Southeast Alaska, serving cruise lines with glacier flightseeing tours and charter air service. The company also handled Delta Airlines ground operations in Juneau. Bob was proud of the more than 120 employees his management team had assembled, as well as the commercial success his company had achieved.

Bob looked comfortable, yet professional, in his normal work attire. He had on a white-collared polo shirt embroidered with the blue and gold Wings of Alaska logo, along with his favorite pair of dark wash jeans. He was just about to make his first phone call of the day when his sister Karen Jacobsen, the company's marketing and cruise tours director, poked her head into the office.

"I'm on my way downtown to check on the tours at the dock," Karen said. "Don't forget we're having dinner at mom's this weekend."

Bob had recruited his older sister to work at Wings early in the company's development. Though she had a husband and three young children at home at the time and wasn't looking to go back to work full-time, Karen's outgoing, friendly personality, incredible work ethic and commitment to customer service were just what the company needed for its growth and Bob convinced her to join the team. Juggling the responsibilities of home, job and working with a family business had become Karen's norm. Even Bob's mother had done a seven-year stint as company bookkeeper in Wings' early years.

"Did you tell Darlene about Sunday?" Bob asked. "I'm not sure exactly when she gets back from her trip to Seattle with the boys."

"Yah, she knows. But put it on your calendar for Sunday afternoon. I'm taking mom to Mass in the morning and you need to come over for dinner, no matter what else you and your wife have going on. Mom really wants us all to get together."

Bob signed a letter on his desk and put it on top of one of his neatly organized stacks. "I'll be there. Thanks for the reminder." He wrote the family dinner date on his desk calendar. "Today's June 22," he thought. "Sunday's the 26th. I need to remember to call Dar and find out when she and the boys fly back from Seattle."

Bob's youngest brother John, Wings of Alaska's Director of Flight Control, joined them in the office.

"It looks like we've got pretty good flying weather today, Bob," he said. "Maybe some light fog and drizzle this morning and I'm thinking we may cancel the first trips out, but the weather should improve and we should be flying soon. I'm headed to the airport dispatch office now and I'll call you when I get there with the latest weather report."

"Thanks, John. I have a finance meeting with John Lucas this afternoon and I plan on being in the office all day. "

"Don't forget about mom's on Sunday," Karen said as John was leaving.

"I'll be there, " he said, looking back at Bob and rolling his eyes and smiling. "Sometimes working with your family has its challenges."

"I love you too," Karen quipped.

Chapter Three

The Last Trip to the Lodge

Rosa Maria Gomar de Vides, a financial planner from Guatemala City, Guatemala, was excited as she and her two children, five-year-old Miguel and seven-year-old Maria, lined up with the other visitors on the dock for their flightseeing adventure. This trip with her children, her mother Rosita, and her mother's best friend Margarette de Munoz, was a dream come true. They were a world away from the weather and topography of Guatemala. The incredible beauty she experienced sailing up Alaska's Inside Passage on her cruise had already touched Rosa's spirit.

"Will I see a big bear?" Maria asked, speaking in Spanish. Her dark brown eyes looked up as her mother lovingly brushed Maria's long, black hair away from her face.

"I want to see a bear, too," Miguel added. "I'm not afraid of bears."

"Well, I'm afraid of bears," said Margarette.

Margarette, Rosa Maria and Rosita all laughed as Miguel, known as Miguelito, and Maria practiced growling at each other like bears.

It was 5:30 p.m. and the Wings floatplanes were lined up along the dock, getting ready to take off for their last tour of the day. It was one day after the longest day of the year, the summer solstice, when it remains light in Juneau until midnight. The weather throughout the day had been changing, especially around the Taku Glacier. While the cloud ceilings and visibility varied, the weather overall remained good for flying. The third week in June was considered the beginning of the peak-visitor season and the Lodge business was already booming.

The dock staff at the downtown Juneau Seadrome Building - the starting point for the Wings Taku Lodge tours - were efficient at organizing people into groups before the flight to the Lodge. They gave each of the groups iconic Alaskan names like Eagle, Orca and Raven, as they calculated the weight of the passengers and made sure every group met the weight and balance restrictions. Rosa Maria's group also included three women in their 60s: Wanda Gard, a retired vision and hearing specialist; her best friend Kathleen Pruneski, a librarian, both from Marshall, Michigan; and fellow World Explorer Cruises passenger Caroline Garner from Portage, Michigan. Donald and Florence Schrantz, an older married couple from Dunkirk, New York, celebrating their second honeymoon, rounded out Rosa's flightseeing group.

Along with George Coulter, Director of Operations Rusty Shaub, and Captains Mike Olsen, James Roe and Kevin Kramer, were scheduled to fly the day's final tour. All of them had been flying with the company for several years and were among some of the most experienced pilots in Southeast Alaska.

Many of the assembled passengers for the final tour smiled as they watched the children playing; bear growls and children's laughter needed no translation.

A Holland America ship tied up directly behind the Wings dock glistened against the emerald green of Mount Roberts in the background. All of the 50 state flags that line Juneau's main road flapped gently in the breeze.

George looked over the passengers assigned to his Otter. Summer dock staff skillfully took the passengers down the long, steep wooden ramp from the wharf to the company's floating docks on the channel. They helped the older passengers board the Otters as George did one final pre-flight check. Once everyone was aboard, George carefully went over the safety briefing and instructed his passengers to put on their seatbelts and the headsets that were available above each seat. Wings planes were outfitted with a recording for visitors that included a safety briefing and detailed history and geography of the area. The recording also pointed out special features of the scenery they would be flying over and gave a brief history of Alaska's capital city.

The children could hardly contain their excitement as their grandmother helped them fasten their seatbelts and adjust their headsets just as the planes' engines began to roar.

When all of the passengers were aboard and the pilots signaled they were ready, the five Otters in the fleet slowly taxied away from the dock and made their way past the giant cruise ships anchored in Gastineau Channel. Princess, Holland America, World Explorer – the big cruise lines made Juneau one of their Alaska stops. Some tied up at the docks while others anchored out in the middle of the channel.

One-by-one the airplanes picked up speed, gently lifting off the water and taking flight. Like a flock of birds, they each followed the lead pilot up and past small boats and giant ships, continuing their flight down the right side of Gastineau Channel, then turning north up Taku Inlet towards Devils Paw.

Rosa Maria sat in the co-pilot's seat on the flight up to the lodge, taking in the breath-taking scenery as the plane's flight path followed the channel separating Douglas Island from the town of Juneau, flying south toward the open water and the Taku River. The 40-minute trip that took them over the lush wilderness of the Tongass National Forest was everything Rosa hoped it would be. The view of the glaciers making up the 1,500-square-mile Juneau Icefield amazed her most. They had seen glaciers from the deck of their cruise ship, but flying over the deep crevasses and seeing the cool blue color of the melt-water pools was stunning. Rosa found herself looking forward to telling the rest of her family all about it when she'd call Guatemala City later that evening. Though Rosa and her husband Byron Vides had recently separated, they spoke on the phone every day. The children loved to share their daily adventures with their father.

Rosa had initially planned the Alaska cruise vacation as a family adventure, but when she and Byron decided to separate, she invited her mother and Margarette to go with her instead. Byron wasn't happy Rosa was taking the children without him, but reluctantly agreed to let them go. Rosa's mother loved to travel any time, anywhere, so Rosita's joining the trip didn't take any convincing. Rosa's brother Miguel often kidded his mom about her passion for international travel, teasing her about dying in some strange place in the world. Miguel wasn't particularly happy about his mom and sister going to Alaska without Byron, but hoped the break from her marriage difficulties would be good for Rosa and a fun adventure for the children.

When George's plane landed 40 minutes later on the Taku River, directly across from the picturesque Hole-In-The-Wall Glacier in front of Taku Lodge, Miguelito and Maria couldn't contain their joy and excitement.

"Watch out for the bears," George said, as he helped the children out of the plane and onto the dock. "They like to lick the salmon oil off the grill outside. And sometimes you can see a baby bear in the trees when you walk along the trail."

"Oso," Maria said to her brother excitedly. "Bear!"

The children ran up the dirt path from the dock toward the lodge, while Rosa Maria helped her mother and Margarette navigate the pathway up the hill.

"It's so beautiful here," she said. "So quiet and peaceful." Rosa looked up to see the distinctive white head and broad wingspan of a bald eagle soaring overhead.

"Si," said her mother. "Muy hermosa."

The members of Rosa Maria's group made their way up the path from the dock to the lodge. The rustic log cabin built in 1923 sat in the center of a large grassy area, the Taku Lodge's covered porch lined with rocking chairs and wooden benches. Flower beds surrounding the building were filled with color. Bright purple lupine was everywhere. The children happily pointed out the large moose antlers attached to the outside of the building. The sweet aroma of salmon cooking on the grill filled the air.

"Tengo hambre," said Miguelito. "Hungry."

***

Entering the lodge, Donald and Florence Schrantz looked as happy and excited as Rosa's children.

"What a beautiful place to celebrate a second honeymoon," Florence said to her husband of 50 years. They had been planning their trip to Alaska for years and were overjoyed to finally be able to be together in this special place, after having had to reschedule their trip several times. Donald, an avid fisherman, hunter, and conservationist, had helped foster the restoration of salmon to Lake Erie. He was an active and respected member of a conservation club where he previously lived in Michigan and where his conservation work earned him the nickname 'Coho Don.'

"I simply can't believe how beautiful it is here," he said. "I wouldn't have thought that after raising four boys and being married for as long as we have, I could be this giddy having this experience."

Florence looked up at Don and smiled. "I guess I made an OK choice when I said yes to you," she joked.

"You think so?" he said, putting his arm around his wife and smiling broadly as he held out a chair for her to take a seat at one of the Taku Lodge's many dining tables. "I hope that salmon dinner tastes as good as they say it is. I'm starving!"

***

As Rosa's group was enjoying dinner in the lodge, George and the other pilots loaded the returning groups of passengers into their planes for the flights back to Juneau and their soon-to-be-departing cruise ships.

George had decided to drop off his returning passengers, fuel his plane and fly back to wait for his last group at the lodge. Wings pilots could choose to spend the between-flight time waiting either in Juneau at the Seadrome or they could fly back to the lodge and wait for their next flight. George loved the peace and serenity of the lodge and often chose to wait there between flights, especially at the end of a long day.

"How was the food today?" George asked some of the returning passengers as they boarded his plane.

"The salmon was fantastic," said one of the guests. "Everything was great. It was a fabulous trip. I went back a few times for more of those yummy cookies!"

"I love those," George said, patting his rather large stomach. "I used to weigh 100 pounds before I started flying up here." George laughed heartily at himself and the members of his return group of visitors smiled. He truly never tired of hearing how much the visitors enjoyed their excursion. He had a real sense of pride in the company and deservedly felt like he had helped shape its success. It bothered him terribly that Bob chose to demote him from Chief Pilot and he couldn't understand his reasoning why.

Chapter Four

The Trip Back to Juneau

After refueling, George returned up the Taku River to retrieve his last group. He enjoyed his time flying alone over the glacier-fed river and marveled at the river's famed Chinook salmon run. After landing and docking, he checked the plane and walked up the hill toward the lodge. He looked forward to having a cup of coffee and spending a few minutes visiting staff in the kitchen while he waited.

That evening, he watched Maria and Miguel chase each other on the lawn in front of the log cabin lodge, while Rosa Maria, Rosita and Margarette gently rocked on the wooden swing on the front porch.

Ken and Michelle Ward had just purchased the historic Taku Lodge. They put their life's savings into turning the historic landmark into one of Southeast Alaska's must-see destinations. They had been working in partnership with Wings of Alaska to fly visitors there for the last year. Ken, a pilot himself, had previously owned his own air-taxi company in Juneau, Ward Air, and Michelle was a long-time Alaska Airlines flight attendant. The Ward and Jacobsen families had a long and respectful relationship.

Michelle had recently purchased several novelty mosquito zappers she kept on the porch that looked like small tennis racquets. The 'zappers' killed bugs with a quick burst of electricity. Rosa's children were having great fun running after mosquitos with the zappers, while chasing each other at the same time. George and Karen never had children of their own, but the kids in their neighborhood loved them both. When George saw Miguel and Maria playing, he grabbed a ball from a toy bin near the porch and started a three-way game of catch with them. The Wards' young children, Mike, Natalie and Buzz, who spent the summer months with their parents at the lodge, joined in the fun for the impromptu game of catch. Though the Ward children didn't know Spanish and the

Guatemalan children didn't understand English, the children had no difficulty playing together.

Wanda Gard and Kathleen Pruneski had also been planning their trip to Alaska for a long time. They had traveled to the interior of Alaska several years before and decided then to come back to see Southeast's mountains and glaciers. While they originally hadn't planned to take the lodge tour that day, Kathleen really wanted to see the view of the glaciers from above so at the last minute they changed their excursion plans. Wanda was happy they did.

Sitting on the front porch watching George and the children play on the grass, Wanda felt an overall sense of wellbeing. She and Kathy had especially enjoyed the Taku River king salmon dinner and she was glad Kathy was able to hike down the trail through the old-growth forest, while she spent her time rocking on the porch taking in the magnificent view.

"Funny how she and the children wanted to see a bear," Wanda thought. "I just love Kathy's curiosity. I guess when you never got to go anywhere or see anything as a child yourself, you just maintain that natural curiosity," she mused. Wanda was grateful she had been able to show Kathy many places since they had become good friends.

Wanda and Kathy first met when Wanda's daughter was a high school senior and a cadet teacher at the Catholic school where Kathy was a teaching nun. Their friendship grew over the years despite the 15-year difference in their age. After Kathy decided to leave the convent and after Wanda's marriage fell apart, Wanda invited Kathy to move in with her.

The blues and purples of the lupine and fireweed juxtaposed against the green of the trees and grass in front of her fascinated Wanda. She could smell the sweet scent of the wild roses and was awed by how close the face of the glacier was to where she was sitting. She marveled aloud to other visitors at the unique blue of the Hole-In-The-Wall Glacier ice.

Kathy and the others returned from their hike shortly before it was time for their group to head back to Juneau. "You just can't describe the color of that glacier," Wanda said to Kathy. "It doesn't look real, does it?" she asked.

"Would anyone like any more of that Russian tea they served?" Kathy asked the group assembled on the porch.

"No thank you," Wanda said, "But if you were going back in, I wouldn't mind another one of those ginger cookies. I wonder if they give out the recipe."

"I'll ask," Kathy said, forcing herself off the comfortable lawn chair she had settled into after her forest hike. "I just love that tea too. Seems like all I have been doing on this trip is eating," she said with a smile as she rubbed her tummy.

"You and me both," Wanda said. "So maybe you should bring me two cookies just in case I get hungry on the flight back!"

The women's banter back and forth had the comfortable warmth of a couple used to teasing each other and laughing at themselves.

Wanda's fellow cruise passengers Donald and Florence Schrantz overheard the women's cookie conversation. "Those cookies are really great, aren't they?" Donald said. A tall man, Donald had an open, friendly face. He had also been thoroughly enjoying his remote wilderness experience.

"I wouldn't mind the recipe either if you get it," Florence said. Florence zipped up the bright red rain jacket she had purchased before her cruise. "It's getting a bit chilly, isn't it?" she asked, turning to her husband.

"I'm so happy we got to take some photos at the foot of the glacier," Florence said. "I can't wait to get them developed and send them back to our boys."

"It is a fantastic view," Kathy agreed. "I'm sure your family will be excited to see the pictures."

"My husband and I had our entire family together just a few weeks before our trip. I wish they could all see how amazing and peaceful this place is," Florence said.

"I think they were jealous we were coming to Alaska without them!" Donald said.

The group laughed again.

"They'd be especially jealous if they knew how great these cookies are," Florence added.

***

George looked at his watch when he heard the distinct roar of an Otter beginning its descent to land on the river.

"Sorry to tell you this folks," he said. "But it's close to your departure time."

George smiled at his young playmates, put down the ball and turned to start down the trail to the dock. "Does anyone need help getting back to the plane?" he asked.

"My mother does," Rosa Maria ventured. "She's tired from all this activity."

"Just let the young folks inside know you want a ride and they'll take care of anyone who needs help," George added.

"Thank you," said Rosa. "And thank you for entertaining the children."

Rosa turned to her children and told them it was time to say goodbye to their new friends.

"My pleasure," said George, as he headed toward his plane. "They're delightful." He needed to do a flight check before the passengers were ready to board. "Last flight of the day. I hope Karen's got something good left for my dinner. And I can't forget to pick up that anniversary gift. I just wish I knew what she wants," he thought.

***

It was close to 8 p.m. when Kevin Kramer helped his last group of passengers onto his deHavilland Otter for the flight. Most would re-board their ship, the *S.S. Universe,* which would depart Juneau at midnight. Kevin loved Alaska's long summer days and was always happy to have a few more hours of daylight to enjoy when he got off work. A sensitive, soft-spoken man who appeared younger than his 30-years, Kevin was a thoughtful, experienced pilot, having flown in Alaska since 1988. He started working for Wings in the spring of 1990 after flying for another air carrier in the region.

Kevin checked the controls one more time and completed his taxi and takeoff checklist. "I'm sorry for the delay folks," Kevin announced. His voice reflected the calm and professionalism Kevin was known for. "It seems one of your fellow passengers decided he didn't want to leave his nice, new rain jacket at the lodge for me to wear, so thanks for waiting for him to go back to get it. Now it's time for your safety briefing, so please give me your full attention, we're ready to take off and I need to remind you about the safety features aboard this aircraft."

After giving the passenger safety briefing, Kevin put his full attention to providing a smooth takeoff from the water, gaining altitude and maneuvering the plane off the river and into the sky. Once airborne, he switched on the pre-recorded soundtrack that detailed what passengers were seeing on the flight and focused on the radio transmissions from the other Wings pilots who were already on the return flight to Juneau.

"Weather conditions and visibility have deteriorated near Annex Creek on the west side of the inlet," lead pilot Mike Olsen radioed to his fellow pilots. There are some low cloud ceilings over there, so we should follow the east shoreline out of the inlet. "

Kevin heard the pilots of the other planes in front of him confirm Mike's transmission and report their positions according to the Wings of Alaska standard flight procedure.

"I'm now at Jaw Point and Cooper Ridge," Olsen reported, "Visibility has opened up and I've got five- to 10-mile visibility and 2,000 foot ceilings. It's good on this side and I'm heading back to the Seadrome."

"This is 336, near Jaw Point," Rusty Shaub reported in. "Ceilings and visibility are substantially better on the east side, as opposed to Annex Creek. I'm headed into Juneau."

"This is 337," radioed James Roe, the third pilot in line. "Visibility low on the southeast shoreline of Taku Inlet, but conditions are much better at Jaw Point. I'm headed in."

"This is 13 Golf Alpha at Taku Glacier and flying downriver," Coulter reported.

Kevin listened carefully to the radio transmissions as he monitored the weather conditions immediately in front of him. He leveled off at 1200 feet over the face of Taku Glacier, and then began flying east toward Turner Lake rather than south toward Annex Creek, following the recommendations of the pilots in front of him. Kevin could see the deteriorating weather conditions towards Annex Creek on the west side of the river. He began to maneuver toward the east shore – standard procedure in case he needed to land on the river to avoid unsafe flight conditions. Just a few miles short of Turner Lake, however, weather conditions on the east side of the inlet improved.

"I've got about five- to seven-miles visibility and about 2000-feet overcast at Turner Lake," he reported. "On my way to Juneau."

***

Although Rosa had occupied the co-pilot's seat on the way up to the lodge, she switched seats with Kathleen for the return trip. Kathleen was open to a new adventure and Rosa was happy to give up the front seat. She wanted to be nearer to her children during the 20-minute- flight.

As he checked his fuel gauges George couldn't help thinking again about not being chief pilot anymore. "I've got more flying know-how in my little finger than these guys have all put together," he thought to himself. "It really does piss me off."

George's thoughts were jolted back to the present by the voices on his headset. He listened on the radio as the other pilots reported that the cloud ceilings and visibility were poor along the west side of the river. He could see that there was better weather on the east side, but decided instead to continue flying down the west side. "I've been up and down this river more than any of these guys," he thought to himself. "I like the west side better."

It was at that point Donald Schrantz, seated across from Wanda, motioned for her to look out the left side of the plane.

"Oh my," she thought. "The fog is really coming in."

There was a slight drizzle and scattered clouds. George checked his altimeter. 1000 feet. "I better go down to 700," he thought.

As his plane neared Flat Point, George looked in front of him toward Annex Creek and could see that the fog was down to the water. He had seen these conditions literally hundreds of times before. He decided the best thing for him to do would be to turn away from the weather and set up for a precautionary landing on the water. George could see the ridgeline behind him from where he had just come with 3000-foot ceilings and 20 miles visibility. He thought he could see the far shore near Turner Lake on the other side of the river, over five miles away, so he turned the plane to the left in an easterly direction and began his descent to land. He checked his altimeter. It read 200 feet.

Chapter Five

Making "The Call"

As Kevin Kramer's plane approached Juneau and began its descent for landing, he started counting aircraft, as he always did, making sure he knew the position on the water of all the planes that had taken off in front of him.

His plane was supposed to be the last in and it was clear that one of the aircraft that should have already landed on the water was missing.

"This is 28 Tango Hotel," he radioed. "Has George landed yet?" He tried to push down the faint anxiety that began to arise and focus on the task in front of him, landing his floatplane smoothly and safely on Gastineau Channel.

Carl Ramseth's job at the airport was to monitor radio transmissions from all the pilots, documenting each checkpoint as the planes passed.

"28 Tango Hotel. This is Carl. No. George hasn't reported in."

Kevin checked his surroundings and re-checked his instruments. "Focus on the task at hand," he thought, as he made his approach. "Land safely, land safely," he thought, as he guided the floats gently onto the water.

"OK, Carl," he radioed as his plane taxied toward the dock. "I'll head back out to take a look just as soon as my passengers deplane."

"Wings base, this is 36," Rusty Shaub radioed. "We're going to head back up the river too. What time and where was the last time George checked in?"

"I heard him at Flat Point around 8:05," Kevin stated.

"O.K. I'm starting the ERP," Carl radioed.

Carl Ramseth always hoped he would never have to make what some flight followers referred to as 'The Call' to activate the company's Emergency Response Plan. Carl looked at his watch. It was exactly 8:23 p.m.

His training kicked in and he immediately took the three-ring binder with the airline's Emergency Response Plan out of the drawer in his desk. He dialed the numbers listed on the plan, first contacting Bob, who agreed it was time to execute the plan, then calling the Alaska State Troopers, Coast Guard, NTSB, and other company officials. He worked his way down the detailed list of emergency procedures outlined for him to follow.

Carl dialed a number he knew by heart, Wings new chief pilot. "Hey Steady, this is Carl," he said. "We have an overdue aircraft with 10 passengers on board," he said, doing his best to maintain his calm. He hoped his voice wouldn't give away the terror he was already beginning to feel and trying to push down.

"George Coulter is in 13GA. He last reported in at Flat Point around 8:05 p.m. but he didn't land with the other planes. He didn't report a problem or anything after that call. Rusty, Mike Olsen and Kevin have already started back up the Inlet to look for them."

Mike Stedman stared briefly at the phone in his hand, hardly able to take in what he was hearing. It was his day off and he had just gotten home from a softball game and was tired and sweaty. He had been looking forward to having dinner and just settling in for the night with a good movie. Mike stared at the picture of his softball team hanging lopsided from a Wings of Alaska logo magnet on his refrigerator door.

"Did you call Jacobsen?" he asked quietly, dreading to have to make that call himself.

"Yes," Carl said. "I'm in the process of notifying all the authorities and we are working through the Emergency Response Plan. Jacobsen also called Bob Engelbrecht at TEMSCO and asked him to launch a search and rescue helicopter. He wants you to meet Engelbrecht at the TEMSCO hangar and go up with him to search."

"I'm on my way," Mike said softly. "Call TEMSCO and let them know I'll be at their hangar in five minutes."

As Mike put down the phone, he quietly said a prayer aloud. "Please God. Let them be OK."

***

Bob grabbed a bottle of water from the small refrigerator he kept in his home office. It felt like his heart was going to come out through his throat and he felt a bit lightheaded as he dialed his sister's phone number. He was glad when Karen, not his niece or one of his nephews, picked up the telephone.

"Hey, Karen, it's me."

"Damn it, I can hardly get through a meal before there's something," Karen thought, setting down the sponge she had been using to clean up after their family dinner.

"Karen, I really need your help right now," Bob said, as calmly as he could muster. Karen's mood shifted. She sensed something different in her brother's tone of voice.

"Coulter's plane is missing and I need you to go to his house and stay with his wife," Bob continued. 'We don't know anything yet. I'll call you as soon as we hear something. Please tell Karen Coulter we'll call you guys first, as soon as we know anything – anything at all."

"Oh my God, Bob. Of course, I'll go right now." Karen's 15-year-old daughter Jeanette looked up from where she was at the dining room table. She could tell something was wrong. She watched the color drain from her mom's face and could see her mother holding on to the edge of the kitchen counter.

"Karen, I haven't called her yet. She doesn't know George is missing and I don't want her to hear something on the radio," Bob said. "We've notified the Troopers and the Coast Guard, so the newspaper or radio folks might have heard something on a police scanner and I really don't want her to hear it first on the radio from Pete Carran," he said.

"It's OK, Bob. Don't worry. I'll handle it," Karen said. "What else can I do?"

"Mom would say, 'Pray,'" Bob said.

Bob could hear the pilots talking to each other on their radios as they headed down Gastineau Channel. "Hey, Karen," Bob added. "Mom's probably asleep now. Let's not say anything to her until we know more."

"Of course," Karen said. "No need to worry her."

"Thanks, Karen," he said. "I've got to go." This was one time Bob was glad he had a sister tougher than he was to support him in the myriad of responsibilities he knew would need to be taken care of.

He was also glad Wings had an Emergency Response Plan to use as a guide for what steps to take next. "It's all on the checklist. Use your checklist," he thought. Bob looked back down at the procedures in the binder that he and other Wings managers kept with them and had practiced and made note of the times and conversations he had.

"State Troopers. FAA. Coast Guard. The cruise line. Ken Ward at Taku Lodge. Director of Operations. Search and Rescue. Bob Engelbrecht at TEMSCO Helicopters." Bob carefully checked to make sure he had written down the time he knew each had been contacted. He stared at the writing on his notepad. "I've got to call the insurance company," he thought. "No. No. Not yet. Let's hope for a good outcome."

His telephone rang again just as he heard Rusty Shaub's voice over the radio. "13 Gulf Alpha, this is 36, do you read me. Over. Come in, George. Over. Wings Base this is 36 at Annex Creek. George, this is Rusty, do you read me. Over. Come in, George. Over."

Bob put his elbows on his desk and held his head in his hands for a moment. "I know I haven't been a very good Catholic boy lately, but let them be OK, Lord. I promise, I'll be better."

The radio crackled again. "One Three, this is 36, do you read me. Over. Come in 13. Over. Wings Base this is 36 at Annex Creek. Thirteen, this is 36, do you read me. Over. Come in, George."

Chapter Six

Glassy Water

Dick Emberton was a year-round employee of Alaska Electric Light & Power Company's hydroelectric plant at Annex Creek. He was tired from a long day and decided going to bed early was a good idea. He put a big log on the fire in the cabin's wood stove and settled in for the night when he heard the sound of airplanes off in the distance. It seemed to him the aircraft noise was coming from further away than normal. "They must be going down the east side of the inlet," Dick thought.

AEL&P was a family-owned utility in Juneau since 1893 run by Bill Corbus. It originally ran on local hydroelectric dams from the area's gold mines and grew to become the largest and only family-owned electric utility company in Alaska. Generations of the Corbus family had been good friends with the Jacobsens.

"It's kind of bad for those guys to be flying out there," Dick thought. He knew well the sights, sounds and natural rhythms of the seasons. He loved working away from the city and though he loved his solitude, he had a positive association with the sounds of airplanes and the summers he spent at Annex Creek. Dick had been to the Taku Lodge many times and knew Ken Ward and the Ward family. He also knew some of the college kids they put to work in summer jobs. He liked them. They were real entrepreneurial Alaskans, he thought.

Dick looked at his watch. Within seconds he heard what sounded like a small explosion. "What the heck was that," he thought, jumping up. Dick listened for a minute and didn't hear anything else. He picked up the phone to call another power company employee working at Annex Creek.

"Did you just hear that?" he asked. "It sounded like an explosion in the movies."

"Yah, what do think it was?" asked his co-worker on the other end of the line.

"I have no idea," Dick said. The men talked for a few more minutes. "It was kind of far away, so it couldn't have been anything here," he said. "I don't think it's worth getting too worked up about. It's quiet now. Probably was a boat engine or something. I'm going back to bed," Dick said. "See you in the morning."

***

Almost a mile from where Dick lay in his warm cabin, George felt the impact as his plane suddenly and unexpectedly hit the water. The next thing he knew the nose of the plane was down in the glassy water of the fog-covered river.

For a brief moment, all he could hear was the ringing in his ears from the boom of the impact and the sound of the plexiglass from the aircraft's front window breaking when the plane hit the water.

He instinctively reached over to check Kathleen Pruneski in the co-pilot's seat. Her head was slouched forward against the control yoke. She wasn't moving. George felt shards of plexiglass around him. He tried frantically to don his own life vest. The 40-degree river water began rushing in through the broken window.

George sensed that the fog must have created flat light conditions that cause the color of the sky and water to appear the same. The water works like a mirror and flat light creates an optical illusion that causes pilots to lose their depth perception and contrast in vision. Though he thought he was 200 feet above the river, he must have lost the visual cues from the hidden shoreline and misjudged his true distance from the water. Glassy water landings, especially in flat-light conditions, can cause pilots to misjudge their height above the water. There had been no time to even radio in an emergency call before it was too late and he found himself covered in shards of plexiglass.

"Grab a life vest," George shouted frantically while brushing pieces of plexiglass from his chest. "Grab a life vest and get out of the plane. Now!" George fumbled with the clasps on his own life jacket. His fingers froze as he attempted to fasten it around him.

"Get out, get out," George yelled again, looking back as the passengers behind him began to move. "Grab your life preserver and get out of the airplane!"

The Otter's engine had broken off the plane and the motor had been propelled backwards under the fuselage, cutting huge holes in the floats. The freezing river water rushed into the cabin from the broken windshield and George could see the water was rapidly flooding down the center aisle. As he turned back around, the front end of the plane separated from the floats. He was momentarily gripped by shock and fear.

"Where are the life vests? I can't reach the life vests," a passenger screamed.

Rosa struggled to get her children's safety belts unlatched. The water level in the plane was already over Miguel's head by the time she was able to get him free from the safety harness. When she finally succeeded, Miguel was coughing and gasping for air.

Rosa grabbed life vests and directed Maria and Miguel toward George in the cockpit. Just then, George heard someone in the back of the plane cry out, "The door is jammed. The door is jammed."

"Follow me. Come out this way, " George instructed Maria, pointing to the pilots window. He looked again at Kathleen in the seat next to him. She wasn't moving and he knew she hadn't survived. "I have to get the back doors open," he thought. "We'll come back for you, Kathleen."

Adrenaline kicked in and something deep within George sprang into action without him taking the time to finish putting on his own life preserver. Maybe it was his training, his protective nature, or maybe it was instinct. Somehow, George pulled himself up through the broken window and maneuvered to the top of the aircraft. He managed to crawl up and over the top toward the tail. What was left of the front of the plane floated downriver.

The airplane had tilted in the water and George dove into the river to reach the handle of the stuck right rear door. He planted both of his feet against the fuselage and pulled as hard as he could. Nothing moved.

George could see two faces on the other side of the door and the water inside the plane had risen to almost the level of their heads. Using every bit of strength he had, George desperately pulled again. This time the door came off.

As soon as she felt the impact of the plane hitting the river, Wanda Gard instinctively grabbed two life preservers, one for herself and another for Kathleen. As she tried anxiously to go to the front of the plane to help Kathleen, the water inside reached waist high and she could see packages floating toward her down the aisle. Other passengers were making their way down the aisle in her direction. Wanda turned back toward the rear door.

She could hear George as he braced his feet against the outside of the cabin and realized that he had somehow managed to climb across the top to the plane's other side. She watched as he pulled the cabin door off completely. Wanda struggled desperately to climb out of the plane. "Oh, Lord," she thought. "I can't do this alone."

The next thing she knew, she was floating in the river.

"George!" she screamed. "Where's Kathleen?"

"I couldn't get her out. I couldn't get her out." Wanda knew in her heart Kathleen hadn't survived. She looked to her side and she saw young Maria floating in the water nearby. She handed Maria her extra lifejacket, thinking it might help her stay higher up above the water.

"Hold on to it," she instructed Maria. "You're going to need it."

Miguel continued coughing and sputtering when they finally got out of the plane and surfaced in the river. Rosa looked around at the wreckage and the people floating nearby her in the silence. She didn't see or hear her mother and felt fairly certain she hadn't made it out of the plane.

George saw Rosa and the children near him in the water. Maria and Miguel were screaming and George saw one of the airplane's severed doors floating in front of them. He pushed it toward the children and then tried to lift them onto it, but every time he tried he wasn't able to keep the door afloat.

Rosa's thoughts flashed for a moment on the feeling of a hand she felt on her back as she was struggling to free Miguel from his seat belt. She wondered if that had been her mother's hand reaching out for help.

"Where's grandma?" Maria cried. "Mama, I'm so cold."

"I know, baby," Rosa said. "But you have to stay strong and hold on. Maria, Miguel we have to pray and stay strong," she said. "I think maybe Grandma didn't get out of the plane, but you have to stay strong and hold on until help comes."

Once again, George tried desperately to lift the children onto the door. The cold water and fighting against the strong river current was claiming what little was left of his strength. He knew they couldn't stay in the water very much longer without the severe stages of hypothermia setting in. Hypothermia occurs when the body's core temperature drops below 95 degrees Fahrenheit. Along with the shivering and mental confusion of hypothermia's early stages, it drains its victims of energy. George knew that death would soon follow. He had no idea how long they had been in the water when he heard what he thought was the sound of a plane overhead. He urgently tried to lift up his arm to signal it. Despite his effort, he knew there was no way they'd be seen through the thick fog.

"Stay there," George ordered the children. "And no matter what, keep holding on to the door," he yelled.

He and Rosa had both spotted another section of the plane floating down the river a few hundred feet away. "I'm going to swim for it and bring it back," he said. Rosa held on to the door with one hand and to Miguel with the other. Somehow, Maria was still managing to hang on to the piece of floating door.

As George swam, the force of the tidal currents in the river pushed against him. It took every ounce of strength he could muster just to barely move forward against the push of the tide.

Wanda Gard noticed the same piece of wreckage George had seen and started to swim toward it as well. "If I don't want to die," she thought, "I have to help myself. My mom and my family need me. I have to conserve my strength." Wanda thought of her mother's dementia and her daughter's multiple scleroses diagnosis. "They need me," she thought.

Slowly Wanda also began to swim toward the larger piece of debris, alternating between swimming and floating when she became too tired. As she tried to see if she could make out the shoreline, Wanda kept slowly swimming and floating toward the debris. "Don't focus on the cold. Keep moving. Don't focus on the cold. Keep moving," was the mantra in her head.

Donald Schrantz had helped Margarette de Munoz get out of the plane. "Please, stay with me," Margarette had begged. "I can't swim." Donald was already in shock. He couldn't see if his beloved wife Florence had gotten out through another door, but he reached out anyway to help Margarette, putting her on his back and helping her exit through the rear of the plane. To Margarette and everyone else, Donald was a hero.

Despite the fog and mist, Wanda thought she could see Margarette and both Donald and Florence Schrantz in the dark water as she struggled to reach the larger piece of floating debris. Donald continued to carry Margarette on his back. Wanda thought she counted eight people in total in the water. She knew it was George trying to swim toward her. He could barely keep his head above the water and she saw that he kept sinking under as he tried to reach the severed float.

"Come on, George," Wanda cried out, wanting to somehow inspire George to keep going. "You can make it." As she sought to encourage George, fear left her and she was resigned to the idea that this might be the end.

George gasped for air. He had heard Wanda's encouragement. As he began to go under the water one more time, he heard a voice inside his head shout, "No! You can't die now. You have to help the children."

George made it to the other side of the float Wanda had reached just a moment before. Several times as he tried to climb on top of it, the float tipped and filled with water. "George," Wanda cried, afraid his efforts would cause the piece to sink. "Please, George just hold on."

Soon after, Wanda saw a group of brightly colored twinkling lights. "I'm so glad I became Christian," she thought. It was the last thing she remembered before passing out.

***

Rosa Maria continued to silently pray. Shivering, confused, grief-filled and afraid, she watched helplessly as her beautiful baby boy Miguel stopped moving and turned blue.

He was gone. Time stood still. There was only the cold, the gray and the silence.

Rosa told herself her baby had only drifted off into sleep. She held him in one arm while she and Maria frantically worked to keep their hold on the floating piece of the airplane door. Together, Rosa and Maria kept trying to move in George's direction toward the larger piece of the plane's float.

George had barely managed to reach the float and knew he didn't have the strength to make it back to Rosa and the children. "It's so cold," he thought. "The children must be so cold."

George and Wanda watched helplessly as Rosa, who was floating in and out of consciousness, let go of Miguel. His tiny body silently floated away on the Taku River and disappeared into the thick, dark-gray fog.

Chapter Seven

The Search

The Alaska State Troopers and the Coast Guard commonly work together on rescues throughout Alaska. Three Wings planes and a TEMSCO helicopter were already in the air searching when the Coast Guard Cutter *Liberty* was dispatched from Station Juneau. The Coast Guard also dispatched its helicopter from Sitka, but that helicopter was more than an hour away.

An Alaska Department of Fish and Game boat, *The Enforcer*, was in the area and joined the search. Lt. Robin Lown and Sgt. Robert Bittick of the Alaska State Troopers chartered a second TEMSCO helicopter and were monitoring radio transmissions. By the time their helicopter deployed, however, the weather had worsened and the fog created a safety concern. The Troopers' helicopter only made it as far as the mouth of Taku Inlet before their pilot made the decision to turn back.

Before the Troopers turned back, Wings pilot Mike Olsen opened an emergency radio channel and radioed Ken Ward at Taku Glacier Lodge.

"Ken, George's plane with 10 aboard is missing," he said. "Can you head downriver in your skiff? We're retracing the flight back toward Annex Creek. There's fog, but I can see through some patches," he said.

"I'm on it," Ken radioed back. He immediately grabbed a lifejacket that was hanging nearby, his coat and two flashlights and within seconds he was headed out the Lodge door.

"Stay on your radio," Ken said firmly to one of his trusted summer workers standing nearby. "We have a missing plane and I need you to monitor the search and rescue from here. You've trained for this. You can do it."

"Paul and Ted," Ken continued, giving orders in the clear, strong manner of a man who had been through crisis before. "Grab some more life vests and flashlights and come with me."

While getting the skiff ready to launch, Ken noticed the calm stillness of the water. It helped steady the anxiety that was creeping into his consciousness about the fate of the plane and its passengers.

"I need you to stay focused, guys," Ken said calmly. "I need your help. These people all need you. You know what to do." Ken, a pilot himself, had a kind and very authoritative presence. He'd lived and worked in Alaska his entire life, and as a pilot knew full well the reality of the present situation and what they might find. Ken's employees, Paul Scriber and Ted Zurdowski, were calmed by Ken's assurances. They worked together to loosen the tie tethering the boat to the dock.

Rusty and Kevin had already landed their planes on the flat, calm water downriver from the lodge near a landmark known to the pilots as Flat Point. Their floatplanes taxied slowly along the river as they looked for any signs of life or debris.

Kevin noticed the distinct color and sheen of oil on the water. "Hey Rusty, I spotted oil on the right side of the bank," he radioed.

"It doesn't look good," Kevin thought, glancing at his watch, hoping they weren't too late. He knew that even if George and his passengers survived a crash, being in the water too long was fatal. Weather conditions continued to deteriorate as his plane slowly and silently floated in the direction of the sheen on the water.

The temperature and dew point had come together and there was no wind at that time in the evening. The water was like a polished glass mirror. Rusty and Kevin each continued taxiing; both having determined that searching from the water level was the safest way for them to proceed in the fog.

Bob Engelbrecht and Mike Stedman were flying in the TEMSCO helicopter somewhat near Rusty and Kevin's position on the water. They were following the shoreline and could see the Wings planes in front of them, taxiing on the river along the west side of the inlet. The pilots remained silent, keeping their emergency channels open, listening and hoping someone would spot George's plane.

Mike Olsen had landed on the river near Annex Creek. Because of the dense fog, he decided to taxi back out of it until he could find a clearing where it would be safe to take off again. He wanted to take off and fly toward the lodge and Ken Ward's position on the river. Having already flown the route several times that night, Mike's gut told him if George's plane had gone down, it had to have been near Annex Creek, the exact place he had advised the pilots following him to avoid less than one hour earlier.

As Mike was flying back toward the lodge, he spotted Ken's skiff on the river and maneuvered his plane near him to land. Ken wasn't in radio contact with the planes and Mike wanted to make sure Ken knew where to search. It only took him a few minutes to land near Ken's skiff.

"Ken, I'm pretty sure they have to be between Flat Point and Annex Creek," Mike said when he reached Ken. "It's the only place they could be but the fog's really thick in there. The four of us came down the east side of the river by Turner Lake and the weather wasn't bad. It's thick fog over by Annex Creek though. I'm going to take off again and fly above it and see what I can find. Rusty and Kevin are already taxiing on the river searching in that same area," he said.

"Thanks, Mike," Ken said. "We'll head down that way. We should pick up radio contact with you as soon as we round Hut Point."

Ken, Paul and Ted watched from the skiff as Mike's plane took off back into the fog. Mike decided it would be best to maintain an altitude slightly above the fog. As he looked out in front of him, he noticed a small opening in the fog and flew toward it. Looking down, he spotted what he thought was debris from the plane floating on the water below. As if peering through a tiny keyhole, Mike then saw George's figure clinging with one arm to a piece of the downed plane's severed float.

Coming in and out of consciousness, George wasn't sure if the sound he had been praying to hear was really a plane overhead, if he was hallucinating or if he was seeing the lights of heaven. In that instant of uncertainty, he asked for forgiveness from God and for forgiveness from Mike and Rusty for not following their directions. Then, summoning one last burst of strength and will, he lifted his free arm from the frigid water in hopes of signaling the pilot.

"There are survivors in the water," Mike radioed excitedly. "Can you read me? Rusty, Kevin can you read me? I've got people in the water."

"I have you in my sight," Rusty said. "Where are you seeing them?"

"They're behind me," Mike said. "I've got people in the water just South of Flat Point. I'm going to land."

"We have survivors. We have survivors," he said into his radio headset to all who were listening. Mike quickly radioed back their exact location, instructing Rusty and Kevin, the Coast Guard search and rescue, Ken Ward in his skiff, and Bob Engelbrecht and Mike Stedman in the TEMSCO helicopter, the location of the wreckage.

"Survivors in the water," Mike repeated.

Chapter Eight

The Rescue

As soon as Mike Olsen spotted the people in the water, Mike knew what he had to do. He also knew the danger he faced landing through the fog.

"Rusty," Mike radioed. "I'm right in front of you. I'm going to need to use you as a reference in landing. I'm about 500 feet and I have plenty of visibility both down and forward at this altitude, but I'm going to have to use your plane as a reference to descend and land through the fog."

"Roger, that." Rusty couldn't see Mike's plane, but he could hear the roar of the old Pratt and Whitney 1340 radial engine coming from directly above him.

Mike could make out several of the passengers drifting in a straight row beneath him, caught in a tiderip. Somehow, using Rusty's plane on the water as a guide, he landed safely through the fog layer onto the water close to where George and Wanda were still barely hanging onto the severed float. He shut the engine down and stepped out of the cockpit onto the Otter's ladder. Mike quickly jumped onto the float, reached out to grab the back of George's coat with one arm, and dragged his more than 200 pounds of dead weight toward him, using all his strength and willpower to pull George into the plane.

"Damn. Shit. What did I do?" George was swearing and screaming incoherently. Mike struggled for what seemed like an eternity to drag George into the plane between the passenger seats.

"Shut up, George," Mike said authoritatively in his booming baritone. "You need to settle down. I have to get the other people."

Mike reached for a paddle that attached to the float and used it to try to grab Wanda, who though unconscious was still miraculously attached to the piece of the downed plane's float that had sustained her.

"Damn it," he thought, unable to hook onto her the first time. He tried again, this time getting hold of her life vest. Mike dragged Wanda toward him and again, with all his strength, tried desperately to lift her onto the float. Exhausted and still unable to do so, Mike held her tightly. Though he couldn't see very far through the dense fog, Mike could hear the sound of Ken Ward's boat engine and knew more help would soon arrive.

"I've got you," he said to Wanda. "Hold on, Ma'am. I've got you. More help is coming. You're going to make it. You're going to make it."

Through the cloud of grey around him, Mike could make out Kevin Kramer's plane drifting toward him. Kevin was also standing on his plane's float, repeating the scene with another woman that Mike had just played out with Wanda. Kevin was trying to pull the woman aboard. The weight of each person's body, coupled with the weight of their wet clothes that were now filled with glacial silt, added to each rescuer's struggle.

Mike yelled in the direction of the sound of the approaching boat engine. "Follow my voice, Ken. I can hear you. I need your help getting this woman into the plane."

"It's OK, Ma'am, you're going to make it," Mike said again. Wanda was coming in and out of consciousness.

A few minutes later Ken Ward's boat pulled up alongside Mike's plane. Without saying a word, Ken, Paul, Ted and Mike maneuvered Wanda's body onto the float and though the doorway and into the plane.

"Mike, take George and this women and head back to town right away," Ken directed. "I'll help Kevin and Rusty. Paul, you go with Mike and help get these two back to the dock."

Mike agreed, hoisting himself into the pilot's seat as quickly as he could. He recognized both his passengers were hypothermic and knew they may not have much longer if they didn't receive medical attention soon. Mike put his headset on and prepared to take off.

Despite the urgency of the situation, Mike took a few deep breaths, slowed himself down and carefully checked his instruments. He took a minute to determine the safest path off the water, still thick with fog. He knew he would be able to radio back to Wings base once he was in the air and gained altitude. He made a mental note to let them know to have at least three ambulances ready at the dock when the planes arrived.

Rusty had been searching farther down the river when he spotted a yellow life vest in the distance and headed in that direction. He quickly came upon an older woman, Margarette de Munoz, piggybacking onto an older man, Donald Schrantz, and somehow Rusty managed to pull them up on to his floats just before Ken's boat arrived. Ken maneuvered next to Rusty's plane and the men quickly repeated the feat of hoisting the survivors through the plane's open doorway.

Quickly scanning his surroundings, Ken noticed a small stuffed eagle puppet floating nearby. He recognized it as one of the souvenirs sold in the lodge's gift shop and realized it might have been purchased for one of the children he had seen playing on the lawn with his own children just hours earlier. Watching the child's eagle puppet float on the water was one of the few memories Ken would ever share with his wife about that tragic evening.

***

As Rosa floated in and out of consciousness in the frigid water, she looked up to the sky above. She knew the river had already taken her mother and both her beloved children and she pleaded with God to take her, too.

Rosa looked up at the gray fog. Her father, who had died three years before, appeared with Rosita, Maria and Miguel in the most beautiful light she had ever seen. They looked happy playing together, singing a children's song the family often sang at family gatherings.

"Why am I here? What's happening to me," Rosa thought. "Why am I still in this water?"

Rosa heard a voice answer her desperate cry to join her family in the light. "Just stop moving your feet," the voice replied.

Rosa listened as her children and parents sang. She tried desperately to stop her feet from treading water, but no matter what command she gave her body, her feet simply would not stop moving.

At that exact moment, Rosa heard a man's voice. Kevin Kramer's plane was on the river next to her. The rear door of his aircraft was open and he was yelling for her to come toward him, but she couldn't move.

Suddenly the vision of her family was gone and Rosa knew she was back in the freezing water. "I can't move," she said softly.

Kevin grabbed a long paddle from the plane. Without waiting for help, he mustered superhuman strength and miraculously managed to pull Rosa out of the river onto the plane's float and then into its interior.

As he took off, Mike could see Kevin's plane below him on the river. He could also see a bright red spot on the river ahead. It took a moment for him to realize that he was seeing the back of a coat on a little girl floating face down in the still water.

It was that moment - and that picture - that would haunt Mike Olsen's dreams for years to come.

***

Mike Stedman and Bob Engelbrecht were still flying the TEMSCO helicopter near Annex Creek.

"This is TEMSCO Helicopter," Stedman called out over the radio. "Rusty, Mike, Kevin. Can anybody read me?"

Stedman was confused as to why no one was responding to his radio calls. They tried several times to reach the other pilots, concerned with the lack of radio response, but hoping at the same time it might mean the other pilots were out of their airplanes and had found the missing plane and passengers.

Flight conditions kept getting worse as they went on. The color of the sky and the color of the water blended together in the evening light. Bob Engelbrecht, one of Juneau's most experienced and skilled helicopter pilots, was concerned about the ugly conditions they were flying into. He knew his limits as a pilot and was painfully aware not to go beyond those limits.

Bob Engelbrecht motioned for Stedman to look to his left. He had spotted debris from the downed plane in the water below. Another minute passed and they were able to confirm that the three Wings planes were already on the water having pulled survivors aboard.

Engelbrecht continued to fly toward Flat Point, where he saw Ken Ward's skiff floating on the river. He spotted a safe landing site and brought the helicopter down onto a large rocky area near the skiff's location. It wasn't long before Engelbrecht and Stedman saw the bodies of a little girl with a red coat and a woman lying in the skiff.

Stedman closed his eyes briefly, fighting to hold back tears. Throughout his almost 20 years of being a pilot in Southeast Alaska, Stedman prided himself on always maintaining his composure. He gulped, focusing on his breathing, struggling to maintain control.

Engelbrecht opened the helicopter door as Stedman continued to look down at Maria's lifeless, tiny frame. Stedman was aware that Ken and Engelbrecht were talking about what had happened, but he couldn't make out what they were saying over the sound of the helicopter blades still rotating.

"I've read a lot about cold water drowning," Stedman yelled, interrupting the conversation. "Maybe we should try to do something."

Ken changed his position on the boat so that he could look directly at Stedman. Mike could tell Ken was also struggling to control his own emotions.

"No, Mike," he said firmly. "There's nothing we can do anymore. They're gone. They're gone."

Chapter Nine

The Dock

Juneau's downtown dock was packed with close to 500 people. Police, EMTs, ambulances and Juneau residents and cruise ship visitors lined the street and upper dock. The weather had deteriorated in Juneau since the Wings pilots had first headed back toward the lodge to begin the search for their missing co-worker and passengers.

A few miles before landing, Kevin Kramer could see one of the Coast Guard cutters just beginning to head out of Juneau to begin its search. The cutter was on Gastineau Channel directly beneath his plane. While he could see them clearly a few hundred feet beneath him, he realized they could hear, but not see, his plane from their vantage point in the fog.

"I must have scared the shit out of those guys," Kevin thought to himself as he passed directly over the Coast Guard cutter. The weather was getting worse by the minute. Despite the lateness of the hour and the deteriorating weather, it was still light outside. Kevin's adrenaline was pumping, so he made sure to check his position in order to bring his plane and passenger safely in for a landing. The moment his plane was secure, the waiting paramedics from the Juneau Fire Department climbed aboard and began administering live-saving support to his now unconscious passenger.

He could see both Mike and Rusty's planes had also landed ahead of him. The Juneau EMTs had several survivors on stretchers and were already carrying them up to the waiting ambulances on the street above.

***

A doctor from the cruise ship was the first to climb aboard Rusty's plane where the two survivors he had picked up, Donald Schrantz and Margarette De Munoz, were in the final stages of hypothermia.

Donald was curled into a fetal position, his body's natural attempt to keep warm.

"Help me take off his wet clothing and lay him flat on the plane's floor," the ship's doctor instructed Rusty. For a moment Rusty hesitated. From what he knew about hypothermia, it was best to allow a person's body to slowly warm and not move the person abruptly and he didn't want to move him, but the doctor was insistent.

"Now," the doctor yelled.

Rusty slowly moved to help, when a Juneau EMT climbed aboard the plane.

"Stop," the EMT yelled loudly, pointing to the ship's doctor as he was moving the patient out of his curled position. "Stop right now," he said. "I'm in charge here. That's not our procedure for hypothermia."

Rusty moved further out of the way and climbed out of the plane through the cockpit door as more EMTs came onboard and prepared to move both of the survivors onto stretchers and into the awaiting ambulances. Looking up, he was shocked to see how many people besides the EMTs, paramedics and emergency personnel were watching from above. He checked to make sure the floatplane was properly secured to the dock and spotted his wife Thyes waiting for him on the loading ramp.

"I sure hope they all make it," Rusty thought, as he made his way up the ramp toward Thyes. When they greeted, the two held onto each other longer than usual.

Thyes spotted Mike and Kevin coming up the ramp and offered to drive all the pilots back to the Juneau airport where they had parked their cars earlier in the day. Normally, the pilots would have flown their aircraft back from the downtown Juneau dock to Wings' airport location to secure them for the night. On the car ride back to the airport Mike couldn't stop talking about seeing the little girl face down in the water. Despite the personal risks they had taken and all that every one of these three men had done to save the lives of their co-worker and the Wings' passengers, each was haunted by the feeling that maybe they could have done more.

Chapter Ten

Prayers and Tears at Bartlett

The emergency room at Bartlett Memorial Hospital was the last place Susan Christianson, a reporter for the Juneau newspaper, wanted to be on her 41st birthday. She knew her husband Steve and her girls, Joy and Sarah, had been planning a special birthday dinner.

"Would it be OK if I use the phone," Susan asked the nurse who was preparing to put an IV into her arm. "I'd like to let my family know where I am. They're expecting me home for my birthday."

"Sure," the nurse said. "Not much fun having pneumonia on your birthday, huh."

Susan informed her husband where she was and asked him to meet her at the hospital later, as she had been instructed not to drive herself home. She handed the phone back to the nurse to return it to its cradle. She laid down on the exam table and the nurse prepared to insert the IV into her vein.

"I hate needles," she said. "Be gentle with me."

"I always am," the nurse replied. Susan turned her face away from the nurse and focused on the activity that was taking place on the other side of the ER curtain.

"What's going on," she asked.

"I'm not sure," the nurse replied. "I heard they're calling in our on-call doctors and extra ER staff. I think there was an accident." Susan had been a reporter for the local newspaper for just over a year. Despite her own exhaustion and shallow breathing, she couldn't help asking questions.

"What kind of accident?"

"Not sure," the nurse replied. "You just lay here and relax, honey. This is going to take a while to drip through. I'll come back and check on you in a bit. Do you need another blanket or anything?"

"That would be great," Susan replied. "I'm feeling kind of cold."

The nurse handed Susan a warm blanket. As she pulled the curtains back to leave, Susan could see several doctors and nurses standing in a line near the sliding doors where the ambulances enter the ER. She thought she could hear the sound of sirens in the distance.

"Something bad is going on," she thought. She turned her gaze to the medicine hanging on the IV pole and watched the liquid slowly drip into the tube attached to her vein. She closed her eyes just as she heard a voice on the hospital intercom announce, "Code Blue."

***

The bag that held Susan Christianson's IV medication was empty. As she waited for a nurse or doctor to come back to release her, Susan kept listening to the frightening sounds of the Code Blue taking place all around her.

She heard a woman's scream, she heard the hushed voice of a doctor giving orders to a nurse, she could make out the low pitched moaning of a man's voice down the hall. She thought she heard someone speaking in Spanish, then the sound of someone crying and the rattle of a hospital bed rolling past her down the hall.

More than three hours had passed before a young nurse – not the one she had seen earlier – pulled the curtains back and stood beside her bed.

"I'm so sorry," she said. "I'm sure you could tell we've been really busy, but we didn't forget you."

"It's OK," Susan said. "What happened?"

"I can't really say much. There was a plane crash." Susan could tell the nurse realized she probably shouldn't have said anything. The nurse quickly changed the subject.

"I have a prescription from the doctor and instructions for you to follow up with your primary care physician tomorrow," she said. The nurse removed the IV from Susan's arm as she spoke, clearly eager to get her out of the emergency room.

"Is someone here to take you home?" she asked.

"Yes, my husband is in the waiting room."

"The doctor asked me to tell you there's no need to deal with any other hospital paperwork tonight. When you feel strong enough, you can get dressed and you're good to go."

Susan thanked the nurse for her kindness. She could tell the woman seemed particularly anxious as she pulled the privacy curtain back around Susan's ER bay.

A few minutes later Susan slowly walked toward the emergency room's waiting area, past the other curtained-off bays. Several doctors were talking quietly in a huddle in the hallway outside an exam area. She noticed two EMTs talking to a Juneau police officer near the sliding glass doors.

Just as Susan entered the waiting room from the patient exam area her next-door-neighbor Karen Coulter walked in from the parking lot. An older man and an attractive woman were positioned on each side of her.

Susan walked toward them. When Karen Coulter saw her, she looked like she was going to faint.

"I'm not here as a reporter, Karen," Susan said, responding to a gut feeling about Karen's reaction to her being there – a reaction she had seen in others before. "I've been here in the ER as a patient myself."

Susan greeted her husband with a hug and apologized for the long wait. The woman with Karen Coulter introduced herself as Karen Jacobsen and the man with them introduced himself as the pastor of the Coulters' church.

Susan knew George Coulter was a pilot with Wings of Alaska. George had kindly flown her eldest daughter, Joy, to the lodge with one of their neighbors for a fun adventure a few weeks earlier. Her children loved George and he was always kind and patient with their questions and interruptions when they saw him outside.

Susan quickly realized George was probably one of the people in the crash. She was almost certain she overheard a nurse say they had taken the pilot up to the ICU, but she wasn't entirely sure she had correctly pieced together the bits and pieces of conversations overheard as she lay in the emergency room for more than three hours.

Karen Coulter sat down on a waiting room chair, while Karen Jacobsen approached the counter to speak to the nurse.

"George is here," Karen Jacobsen said upon returning from the desk, kneeling in front of her and gently taking Karen Coulter's hand, "but they can't tell us anything more about his condition just yet."

"Can I go back to see him?" Karen Coulter asked.

"They'll let us know as soon as you can," Karen Jacobsen said. She had a warm, calm demeanor and Susan noticed the reassuring sweetness of her tone-of-voice. "They're running some tests now, but he's alive, Karen."

"What can I do to help," Susan asked.

"Please pray for George and all the other people," Karen said, her eyes filling with tears.

"Of course we will," Susan replied. She sat down in the open seat on the other side of Karen Coulter and listened as Karen's pastor quietly asked Jesus to bless and watch over all those who had been on the plane and those who were caring for them.

A few minutes later a nurse signaled the go-ahead for Karen to go back into the exam area.

Susan gave her neighbor a hug and watched as all three disappeared through the door and down the hallway. Before she and her husband were able to leave the waiting room, several other people Susan recognized as being Wings or cruise line employees came into the area.

"Aren't you a reporter," one of the young women asked nervously as Susan and her husband walked past them. Susan smiled and shook her head.

"No," she replied. It was at that moment that Susan decided to quit her job as a reporter for the Juneau Empire. "Life's too short and too precious to feel like I'm preying on people's tragedies," she thought to herself. "I'm done."

"No, I'm not," she said, turning away from the group and walking toward the exit.

"I'm exhausted, Steve. Let's go home. It's been a really long day and a birthday I will never forget."

Chapter Eleven

June 23: Do Unto Others

Bob Jacobsen's alarm went off at 4:30 a.m. He managed to get a couple hours of sleep. As he rolled over in bed, the events and emotions of the previous night came roaring back into his consciousness.

Bob made mental notes of the tasks he'd need to face in the day ahead, including calling his wife to let her know about the accident. He hoped to go to the hospital first to check on George and to meet the survivors. He dreaded facing them and talking to the families of the victims. "How can I comfort them? What can I even say?"

Bob turned the shower on full force. As the warm water washed over him Bob's grief finally caught up. He grabbed the shower wall to steady himself and keep from falling. His entire body shook with the overwhelming weight of his sadness.

***

About 5:30 a.m. Bob pulled into the parking lot of Bartlett Memorial Hospital. When he entered and told the emergency room nurse who he was and why he was there, the nurse directed him to the Intensive Care unit where George, several survivors, and some Wings and cruise ship employees had remained throughout the night. The first person he recognized was Kieran O'Farrell, a Wings pilot, who had stayed at the hospital all night to be a liaison between Wings and survivors' family members.

"I'm so sorry, Bob," Kieran said softly, greeting Bob outside the ICU waiting area. Kieran had flown all day on the day of the accident. She had left the Lodge with her own last group of passengers shortly before the final group took off. As Kieran departed the downtown Seadrome dock ferrying her Cessna 206 back to the airport, her background training in meteorology made her especially concerned. With the light mist developing and the temperature and the dew point coming together, she worried the weather could deteriorate and create dangerous flying conditions.

When George's plane was reported missing, Kieran's friend and colleague, pilot David Fredericks, came to her house to let her know what was happening. Dave had also flown all that day, piloting the company's scheduled routes to the West. Dave's first thought after hearing the news of the accident was to pick up Kieran to see if there was anything they could do to help. The two then returned to the Wings' dispatch office where they heard on the radio that their coworkers had found survivors and were returning to Juneau. Kieran decided she would go to the hospital to provide support. She could never have imagined how that decision would impact her own life.

"Thank you so much for being here all night, Kieran. I don't even know where to start."

Kieran gave Bob an update on the survivor's conditions. "I'm not sure if anyone told you that Mr. Schrantz – the man from New York who Rusty rescued - died of a heart attack last night on the dock, shortly after the ship's doctor mistakenly tried to move and treat him in the plane. The EMTs tried to save him, but he was officially pronounced dead when they brought him into the hospital," Kieran said.

"Yes," Bob said, looking down. "My sister Karen called me and kept me in the loop on what was going on here at the hospital. I wanted to come last night, but I was dealing with the Coast Guard and Troopers." His voice trailed off.

"The cruise ship people have been here working with the survivors and the police to contact family members," Kieran said after a brief silence.

"Yes, I've been working with them to arrange for any family members who can, to fly here," Bob replied.

"I spent time last night with an older lady from Michigan who survived. Her name is Wanda Gard. She lost her friend, Kathleen Pruneski, and was asking about her all night. I'm so glad I was here. Wanda kept asking me not to leave," Kieran said. "She was absolutely terrified, freezing cold, crying and kept asking me if we knew what happened to Kathy. From what I've heard, they haven't recovered her body."

Kieran looked down at her hands. She was thinking about how she had tried to help stop Wanda's seemingly uncontrollable shivering by climbing into the hospital bed with her and holding her. "She was just so cold," Kieran said aloud.

Bob remained silent for a moment. "I'm so grateful you were here for her," Bob said softly. "I'm sure it wasn't easy."

"Wanda kept saying 'I'm all alone,' and all I could think to say was that she wasn't alone, that everyone here was so sorry for her loss and that we were all there for her," Kieran added. Bob stood quietly, again, watching Kieran lost in her own thoughts as she held back tears.

"I understand that George had some heart issues going on last night," Kieran continued. "Besides Wanda Gard, the two women they rescued from Guatemala only have minor physical injuries. I understand some bodies were recovered at the scene last night, including the little girl from Guatemala and another woman, but I don't know who that was."

"That's right," Bob said, waiting a moment to see if Kieran had any more she wanted to share. Of all his employees, Bob considered Kieran the most conservative of the about two-dozen pilots working for Wings. They had at times disagreed on weather conditions being good enough to fly, but Bob and Wings management always respected Kieran's position and never pushed her to fly in conditions she considered unsafe. Kieran respected Bob and the other managers' commitment to honoring her and other pilots' individual flight decisions, even when they disagreed.

"I'd like to see George and each of the survivors," Bob said. "Then I plan to head to the office to work with the Coast Guard on recovering the plane and any victims that might still be onboard," Bob said. "Kieran, I am so grateful for what you did staying here overnight and helping."

Kieran handed Bob a piece of paper with the patient room numbers and the name of the nurse in charge. "The nurse asked us to check with her first to make sure it's OK to go in to see people. Do you want anyone to go in with you?" Kieran asked, pushing her emotions down and coming fully back to the present moment.

"Thanks, Kieran. No," Bob replied. "Karen is on her way back to the hospital soon and she's organized a group of Wings people to work with the ship's folks to make sure the patients have everything they need. You should go home now and get some sleep. We're planning to have our employees get together at the hangar early this evening to talk about what just happened. Someone will let you know the time."

Bob looked at the paper with the room numbers of the survivors Kieran had handed him. They said goodbye and Kieran watched as Bob slowly walked toward the nurses' station. His sadness and anxiety were visible to her, in spite of his attempt to be strong.

***

Rosa Maria Gomar de Vides was partially sitting up in her bed when Bob entered her room. It was just before 6 a.m., less than 10 hours after the accident.

"Mrs. Gomar de Vides," Bob said softly, introducing himself as he pulled a chair up next to her bedside. "I'm Bob Jacobsen. I'm the President of the airline company that took your mother and your children."

"I'm so sorry," he said. "I know there is nothing I can say to ease your pain, but I want you to know that we will do absolutely everything we can ...." Bob's voice trailed off.

Rosa turned her head toward Bob and gently reached out to take his hand.

"You didn't take my children and my mother," Rosa said. "God took them. And now they are playing in God's house."

Chapter Twelve

We Can Find That Plane

Bob's older brother Jim Jacobsen, a captain for Alaska Airlines and one of the owners of Wings of Alaska, was getting ready for work at his home in Issaquah, Washington, when he received a call from his next-door neighbor Stew Cogan. It was 6 a.m. and Jim knew right away something must be wrong for his neighbor to call so early.

"Jim, I hate to tell you this if you haven't already heard, but I was listening to the news and there was an aircraft accident in Juneau last night. Apparently there were 10 people on the plane. There were some survivors but also some fatalities, " Stew said. "The name of the airline wasn't mentioned in the news."

Jim knew that Wings was the only air carrier in the area with 10 seats on board its planes. "My God," Jim said. "I haven't heard. Thanks for letting me know, Stew. I'll call my sister right now."

Jim knew his brothers and sister had to be swamped in the immediate aftermath of a fatal accident. He called his sister's house even though it was only 5 a.m. in Alaska. Karen's husband, Jeff Hansen, answered the phone. They spoke for a few minutes and Jeff filled him in on what he knew about the status of the accident, the survivors and the victims.

"Jeff, I'm going to call Bob right now and tell him I'm going to take time off work and come up to do what I can to help. Please let Karen, John and mom know I'll be on the first flight out of Seattle. I should be there by early afternoon."

"Thanks Jim," Jeff said. "I know they'll all appreciate you being here."

Jim was a "pilot's pilot" and a hero for many people at Alaska Airlines. He had managed to safely pull a jet he was flying out of what people in the airline industry had said was an un-survivable wind shear event that happened shortly after takeoff from the Juneau airport on January 29, 1993. Wind shear is a large variation in wind velocity and direction that exerts an extreme force on the aircraft. Jim had managed to pull his airplane out of it, saving himself, his three crewmembers and the 31 passengers aboard.

When the aircraft was safely at altitude cruising toward Seattle, Jim turned control of the aircraft over to his first officer, came out into the cabin and spoke to every passenger onboard, providing reassurance and comfort through his professionalism and presence. He knew firsthand the impact accidents and traumatic events have on passengers and employees and he wanted to make sure Wings was able to organize counseling and other needed services for its pilots and employees. Though he wasn't involved in any of the day-to-day Wings operations, as one of the owners he felt responsible. And as a member of the Jacobsen family, he had been brought up to do whatever it takes to help – no matter what. He knew Bob would have to focus on a myriad of details with the FAA, Troopers, cruise ship companies, survivors and victims' families.

"My Alaska Airlines incident happened on a Friday night and I didn't sleep until Tuesday," Jim thought. "I had so much adrenaline going through my body and I hurt so much, I had to crawl up the stairs that first night. They've got to be hurting too."

As Jim made preparations to call in and take time off of work, he couldn't help but think back to the trauma that he, his flight attendants and others had experienced after his wind-shear incident and the lack of help they received at the time. This was by no means the fault of Alaska Airlines. None of the major or regional airlines had come to the realization in 1993 that you don't need bent metal and broken bodies to have severe trauma after an incident causing post-traumatic stress. Fire departments, police and first responders had come to that realization and had taken action. They had begun to use de-briefers and counselors after traumatic incidents to help their employees with great success.

Shortly after Jim's incident, the husband of one of his flight attendants called him late at night, afraid his wife might commit suicide. Jim's reputation at the airline was also due to his unflinching support of his co-workers. The morning after he received the call from the flight attendant's husband, Jim went to Alaska Airlines' chief pilot and the Vice President of Flight Operations and pleaded with them to get counseling for his flight attendants. Management realized then that something needed to be done. The chief pilot arranged for a mental health professional from the Seattle Fire Department to do a de-briefing. The only stipulation was that all four crewmembers must be present. This presented a bit of concern for Jim and his first officer. At that time, pilots could not receive mental health counseling without risking losing their medical certificate. The counselor understood their situation and stated she was not counseling the whole crew, just the flight attendants, but she wanted all the crew members to participate.

With the insistence of two fellow pilots at Alaska Airlines, Mike Reinhardt and Bill Morin, Jim and his crew made a video about coping with trauma after an incident. Mike and Bill convinced the crew that making the video would help other crews that are involved in "out of the ordinary" situations. When the video was complete, they showed it to the VP of Flight Operations and the CEO of Alaska Airlines at the time, Pat Glenn and Ray Vecci. Their immediate response was, "The checkbook is open, what do we have to do?" With that, the Critical Incidence Response Team was created, totally funded by Alaska Airlines and staffed by trained employees. Jim was in the first class of 30 trained crewmembers and long considered the team's formation as his greatest contribution to the aviation community.

"I wonder if Alaska Air has names of any professionals in Juneau who could help our Wings employees," Jim thought, coming back to the present moment. "Man, this doesn't ever get any easier."

***

From the time Bob entered the office the morning of June 23rd his phone never stopped ringing. He was barely able to push down the reality of his earlier hospital visits, when local, national and international newspapers, radio stations, the FAA, the police, and the cruise lines began to call with questions and things he had to take care of. There were the supportive calls and faxes too, from colleagues, friends and family. Bob appreciated getting a call from his brother and knowing he was on his way to help with whatever he could. He tasked Karen and his office staff with organizing an employee debriefing session that included counselors and to develop a plan to offer further individual counseling to anyone who wanted it. He worried if, and when, the pilots and the company would be ready to fly again. Bob had voluntarily suspended all flight operations that day, and wondered how, when or even if they would be back in business.

"Take things one pitch at a time," Bob kept telling himself. "One pitch at a time." Bob looked at the clock on his wall. It was shortly after 11 a.m., less than fifteen hours since the accident occurred.

The phone rang yet again. It was a call from the U.S. Coast Guard 17th District Command in Juneau. Bob listened attentively to the voice on the other end of the line, almost unable to fully process the content of the information being relayed.

"O.K, thank you for letting me know." Bob said, putting the phone down in its cradle. Sitting alone at his desk, Bob felt sick to his stomach.

"How can the United States Coast Guard give up searching for our plane and four missing victims after less than 15 hours," he thought. "I can't believe it."

A few moments later Bob looked up when he heard a knock at the office door. It was longtime Juneau City Assembly member and family friend Errol Champion. Errol was loved and respected around Juneau for his warmth, friendliness and community service.

"Bob," Errol said, slowly sitting down in the chair facing Bob's desk. "Tell me how I can help."

"I don't even know what to say, Errol. I'm in absolute shock. I just got off the phone with the Coast Guard. It's less than 15 hours after the accident and they just told me they're giving up searching for our plane and the bodies that haven't yet been recovered. They said our wreckage is in more than 150 feet of river water and glacial silt and there's no way anybody can ever get to it."

"Wow," Errol said, sharing in Bob's shock and disbelief. "That is hard to believe. You guys rescued the survivors and now they're already giving up searching for the bodies and the plane?"

"I can remember in 1972 when they searched for the airplane that Congressmen Hale Boggs and Nick Begich went down on. I think close to 100 military and civilian airplanes spent nearly 40 days looking for them. How is it even possible that they're giving up your search so soon?"

Bob looked directly at Errol. "I was president of the Juneau-Douglas High School student body when that accident happened and my buddy Drew was senior class president. We both were into politics and had arranged to have Begich and Boggs speak to the high school. We were their first stop after arriving in Juneau that morning and the entire student body was waiting in the high school auditorium when we learned their aircraft didn't arrive and was missing."

"It's just crazy the Coast Guard called off the search for the missing," Errol said again, shaking his head. "I can't believe how messed up that is."

It might have been Errol's kindness and warmth, but in that moment Bob felt overcome with gratitude for his friend's presence and comforted by having someone he respected confirm his shock over the Coast Guard's actions. Errol was a commercial pilot himself and had been a manager for one of Southeast Alaska's largest heavy equipment companies, NC Machinery. He currently managed Silver Bay Logging, a helicopter logging company with both helicopters and fixed-winged aircraft in its fleet. Bob knew Errol had been through tragic accidents in his own long career.

Errol sat quietly for a moment, deep in thought.

"Bob, I've got a river boat and a strong kid. My boat has a new GPS with sonar. Bill Corbus and I know that river like the back of our hands. Let us help you find the plane and the victims, Bob," he said. "Let us help."

"We have to bring those people back to their loved ones," Bob said, looking into his friend's eyes. "We just have to send them home. The families need funerals. We have to try."

"We'll help you bring them home," Errol said. "We can find that plane."

***

As soon as she saw Errol leave, Karen knocked quietly on the door of Bob's office.

"I'm sorry to bother you, Bob, but the Anchorage newspaper wants to talk to you about what's happening. Ralph Thomas, a reporter from the Anchorage Daily News is on the phone. Can you take it now?"

"Sure," Bob said. "Do you think I should tell them that the Coast Guard gave up searching for the missing victims?"

"Wow, Bob, that's a shock," said Karen. "I don't know what to tell you except trust your gut. Maybe that's why he's calling."

"Ok," Bob said. "Put the call through."

***

At Karen Jacobsen's request, Bill Pratt, a Juneau counselor with a reputation for working with first responders, visited George Coulter and the other survivors at the hospital on the afternoon of June 23rd.

"I'm sorry about what happened, George," Bill said, sitting down next to George's hospital bed, "but everyone is so glad you made it through the accident. Karen Jacobsen asked me to stop by the hospital today to check on you. I don't know if you remember me, but I'm a counselor here in town and I'm going to be helping out at a meeting tonight at the Wings' hangar. Everyone's concerned about how you are doing George," he said gently.

"Not too good," George said. "I just keep thinking about how the accident happened. I guess I didn't listen to Mike and Rusty soon enough about going down the other side of the river. I was so stupid."

Bill reached out to help George adjust the nasal cannula that was supplying him oxygen. Bill had been told the doctors were concerned about George's heart and didn't want George to become agitated by thinking about the accident.

"George, from what I hear," he said calmly, reassuring him, "you did everything you could to help the passengers. All you need to think about right now is getting well and how happy your wife, your friends and everyone at Wings are that you survived."

"Thanks, Bill," George replied. "Today is Karen and my wedding anniversary. I never expected to celebrate it from a hospital bed."

Bill stayed silent for a moment, carefully selecting his words. "I spoke with Karen before I came here," he said, "and from what I can tell, Karen feels so grateful and blessed to have you here to be able to celebrate many more anniversaries together."

George's eyes filled with tears. "Everything happened so quickly."

"There's plenty of time to talk about what happened later, George. Now is the time for you to heal and for you to focus on your recovery."

"Thanks, Bill. Will you do me a favor though?"

"Anything, George. How can I help?" Bill asked.

"You mentioned going to the hangar tonight. Will you give Rusty and Mike a hug for me when you see them and tell them I'm sorry." George gazed up at the ceiling, then slowly turned toward Bill. "Tell them I'm so sorry."

"Of course, George," Bill said. "Get some rest now and I'll be back to see you later. And George, please know that I'm here for you anytime. I'm going to leave my card with your wife in case you want to call, OK?"

Having worked with trauma for many years in his practice, Bill knew George's road to recovery, both physically and emotionally, would be a long one. He hoped George would have the strength to find his way to move through the pain.

"I'll see you soon, George." Bill said. "I'll send your wife in now. She's been very patient and kind to let me come in!"

George smiled. "She's my rock," he said.

Chapter Thirteen

The Chicken Pox

Terri Sagmoen and Darlene Jacobsen had been best friends since they met at West Seattle High School.

Darlene hated leaving Juneau in the summer, especially with it being Wings' busy season. She was happy, however, to have the chance to take her boys, three-month-old Christian and four-year-old Nathaniel, to Seattle to visit her family and friends. She planned to leave Seattle to head back to Juneau earlier that week, but Christian was fussy and clearly not feeling well when Darlene noticed a few spots on his tummy.

"I can't believe the doctor said you have Chicken Pox," she thought as she gently rocked her baby boy. "I guess poor Terri has to put up with us for a few more days until you're well enough to travel."

Although Darlene never thought of herself as particularly pretty, Bob considered himself really lucky to have such a beautiful, smart wife. His brothers and sisters loved to tease him for 'marrying up' and he secretly felt proud knowing his friends envied his 'catch.' Darlene's sense of adventure, her love of Alaska's outdoor activities and her natural beauty drew Bob to her from the first time they met. Darlene stood out in the crowd without even trying. Her makeup routine consisted of lip-gloss and mascara. Bob loved how Darlene's blue eyes seemed even bluer when she smiled and how when she laughed it felt like she was laughing with her soul. And Bob was continually in awe of what an incredibly devoted mother Darlene was to their boys and how kind and engaged she was with all the children and families they knew.

Darlene first came to Alaska not long after graduating from high school. She attended an airline course at Highline Community College in Seattle and was among a group of women hired by Alaska Airlines to come to work in Juneau, where she worked as an agent for more than 20 years before retiring after Christian was born. Darlene also worked part-time at Wings before the children were born, helping grow the family business.

Darlene brushed a few wisps of hair off her face, trying not to disturb Christian. Nathaniel played quietly with his toy trucks and planes on the floor. "I'm hungry, Mom," he said.

"Hey Buddy, give me a few more minutes so I can get Christian to sleep and we'll go downstairs and get you something," she whispered. "You're being such a good big brother. I can't wait to tell your Dad what a great traveler you've been."

Darlene made a mental note to make one more shopping trip to Seattle's Southcenter Mall before heading home to Juneau. "I really need to get something special for Nathaniel to play with on the plane," she thought.

Darlene looked down lovingly at Christian, feeling grateful and blessed that he was starting to feel better, despite his Chicken Pox. "I hope you sleep well, my beautiful baby boy," she thought.

***

Terri was thinking about what to make for her family, Darlene, and the boys for dinner and only half listening to the car radio as she inched her way home from work in Seattle's infamous rush hour traffic.

The words "Wings of Alaska" and "crash" on the radio suddenly jolted her fully back into the present. She stared at the radio in disbelief.

"The Coast Guard deployed a rescue helicopter but authorities are unable to provide further details regarding the fate of the passengers or pilot at this time," the news announcer said.

"Oh no," Terri thought. "God, I hope Bob's OK. The accident happened last night. I'm sure Darlene must already know."

Terri had flown with Wings of Alaska many times and had been to the Taku Glacier Lodge with Bob and Darlene on her many visits to Juneau. She could picture the route the flights took along the Taku River, knowing full well the horrible impact a crash could have. Terri's end-of-the-day tiredness and the triviality of her problems quickly vanished. "I have to just be there for Darlene and the kids," she thought, hoping Bob was OK and praying Darlene wouldn't have heard about the accident on the radio.

Terri arrived home soon after to a quiet house. She knew Darlene would be upstairs and slowly headed up, not quite knowing what to say or how to act. Darlene was walking down the hallway toward her from the bedroom and Terri couldn't hide the anxiety she felt in her gut since she first heard the news.

"What's wrong, Terri," Darlene asked. "Is something wrong?"

Terri knew at once that Darlene hadn't yet heard the news. She couldn't imagine what Bob was going through, however, she knew Bob well enough to know he had to be overwhelmed with his responsibilities in the moment and probably didn't want to further worry his wife, who was already dealing with their sick infant.

"Darlene, you need to call Bob right away. I'm so sorry but I heard on the radio that Wings had an accident."

Darlene stopped in her tracks and grabbed the hallway wall. "Is Bob OK? Oh, my God, what happened?"

"I don't know, Dar," Terri said softly. "I'm sure he's OK. Nathaniel, come with Terri and let's get a treat for you in the kitchen."

Nathaniel looked up at his mother. "It's alright," she said. "Let Aunt Terri get you something to eat. Mommy is going to call Daddy, OK?"

Terri took Nathaniel's hand and gently guided him toward the stairway.

"Call Bob," she said, looking over her shoulder at Darlene. "Use the phone in my bedroom."

Chapter Fourteen

Boats, Brothers and Body Bags

Matt Roys grew up just around the corner from the Jacobsen family. He always considered John his best friend and thought of John's mother Jerry Jacobsen like a second mother. The Roys and Jacobsen families were friends for more than 50 years. Matt and John spent hours playing baseball at the Juneau rock dump and hanging out as children and teens. John was the youngest Jacobsen child, and both he and Matt often talked about how they enjoyed growing up with the kind of freedom and connection to the outdoors that small-town Alaska provided.

Although he had first worked for Wings as a dockhand and later trained to become an aviation maintenance technician, Matt had left the company and spent the winter traveling with his wife Sharol and their two-year-old daughter. They were driving back to Alaska after spending time in Montana, when his wife was suddenly overcome by a horrible feeling that something was wrong.

"Nothing's wrong, honey," Matt said, as they pulled into a campground to spend the night.

"It's weird, but I just get these feelings," Sharol said. "I just wish the radio worked better all along the Alaska Highway."

Matt turned the dials on the car radio, searching for any station he could find to pacify his wife.

Frustrated, Sharol pushed Matt's hands aside. "Let me try," she said. Static from the radio continued for a while as Sharol played with the dials. Suddenly, they heard just one sentence clearly come through.

"Airplane crashes in Taku Inlet and seven are dead."

Then nothing. Just static.

"That's really weird," Matt said.

"I told you something was wrong," Sharol said. "I told you I had a feeling! Who do you think it is?"

"Look, honey, there's nothing we can do about it from here. Let's just put up the tent and get settled in for the night."

When the family finally made it to Skagway, Matt went directly to the Wings of Alaska office located there. Wings had been expanding its commuter airline service with scheduled flights and Skagway was one of its regular destinations. As soon as he heard what had occurred from one of his former co-workers, Matt called his old friend John to check on him.

Sharol stood nearby and watched her husband's face turn white as he listened to the voice on the other end of the phone.

"Of course, I'll help," Matt said. "I can fly out of here on the next fight and be there whenever you need me. Ok. Ok, no problem. Bye. I'll call you when I get to Juneau and you can pick me up." Matt hung up the phone and looked at his wife and daughter.

"I'm sorry, honey," he said. "I've got to go. Johnny needs me to help them out. He told me that the Coast Guard gave up looking for the plane that went down and there are still missing victims. He said the Jacobsens decided to keep trying to find the plane on their own."

Matt had served in the military where he received his mechanical and aviation training. He knew what a search like the one the Jacobsens were organizing meant. If they were lucky enough to even find the airplane, Matt's military experience had taught him the horrible reality of seeing death up close. He knew his friend John would need his support.

"Of course, you have to go and help," Sharol said. "We'll be OK. We can get the car on the ferry ourselves and meet you back at home. We're Alaskans, right? It's what we do."

***

By the time Jim Jacobsen arrived in Juneau early that afternoon, Errol Champion was developing a plan to go out and search for the downed plane. On June 23, there were extreme tidal variations in the Taku Inlet. Errol consulted with Jim, Bob and others to further develop a strategy for finding the downed plane and victims.

John and Matt were to head out the next day on the Jacobsen family's Bayliner, a 28-foot pleasure craft. Mitch Falk would join them aboard his flat-bottom landing craft, the *Gumption*. Mitch Falk's business was transportation on the water. In Southeast Alaska everything moves from place-to-place via air or water. Despite a busy schedule of hauling freight to Gustavus, other Southeast towns, mining and fish camps, Mitch dropped everything when he was asked to help and made plans to join the Wings recovery efforts.

Errol Champion and his 18-year-old son Evan would be on Errol's boat, which had the sonar. Also joining the search was Bill Corbus, in his 18-foot skiff. Bill was able to provide ropes and grappling hooks that could be used to snag the plane if found. Mike Stedman, Wings' Chief Pilot, also joined the search along with a number of other community volunteers.

Longtime Juneau fisherman Wayne Alex would later join the group with his purse seiner, the *Pacific Bell*. A seiner is a 58-foot fishing vessel that has a large boom and power block that uses a wall of netting to encircle an entire school of fish. The ropes attached to the netting then pull the net together like the drawstring of a woman's purse.

Another longtime Jacobsen neighbor, fisherman Scott McAllister, would also join the team aboard his purse seiner, the *Owyhee*. Pete Lind and Dick Callahan from Commercial Dive Services would join as divers. Allen Shattuck, another family friend whose company was also the insurance agency for Wings of Alaska, volunteered to pilot the Jacobsen family's 24-foot work boat, a Reinell. Wings planes would be made available to help search from the air.

Bob personally took on the unenviable task of getting body bags from the Alaska State Troopers. "I can't live with not bringing those victims back to their loved ones," Bob told John and Karen that evening, as plans for the recovery were being finalized.

"None of us can," Karen said. "We're doing the right thing, Bob. We'll find them.

Chapter Fifteen

Finding Out and Waiting

Dennis Schrantz, the second oldest of the four Schrantz brothers, was on a business trip and had just gotten back home to Michigan when he answered a phone call from his youngest brother.

He could tell something was wrong. "Den, I have been trying to get ahold of you for hours," Timmy said anxiously, when he heard Dennis' voice. "Something terrible happened. I don't even know how to tell you."

Dennis sat down on his bed and took a slow deep breath. "It's OK, Timmy. Just tell me. What's going on."

"Mom and Dad were in an airplane crash in Alaska and they're both dead." Timmy's voice cracked as he spoke.

"Are you kidding me?" Dennis was shocked. This couldn't be happening.

Dennis remembered a premonition he had a few days before his parents left for their trip. He had a vision of them on a small plane that exploded in the air. Dennis was so upset by what he saw that he took the unusual step of calling his dad to find out what kind of plane they were going to be flying to Alaska. Donald assured him the only plane they were flying on was the jet that took them from New York to Seattle to join their cruise ship.

"They weren't supposed to be on a small plane," Dennis said. "They weren't supposed to fly on anything but the jet to Seattle and back." Dennis stared ahead at a painting on the wall.

"God, Den, I wish it wasn't true," Timmy said. "Joe's been in touch with the cruise line and the Alaska State Troopers. And he talked to the owner of the airline." Joe was the eldest of the four Schrantz brothers.

"All we know is that they decided to take a floatplane tour over some glaciers to a remote lodge outside Juneau and they crashed into the river on their way back to the ship," Timmy said.

"They said Dad was found alive and flown back to Juneau by one of the float-plane pilots, but that he died of a heart attack and the effects of hypothermia," Timmy continued. "But the worst part is they haven't found Mom's body. They think she might have gone down with the plane."

Dennis' eyes welled with tears. He tried not to picture his dear mother's body under the water, alone at the bottom of a cold, dark Alaskan river.

"Den, I know this is awful to ask right now, but we want you to call Mom's brothers and sisters to tell them what we already know. All the kids decided a couple hours ago, when we couldn't reach you, we should all head to Mom and Dad's house with our families and wait there together until we can find out more information. Joe thinks it would be good to all be together."

The Schrantz family was raised Roman Catholic, although Dennis had never described himself as a religious person. He did, however, have a strong spiritual belief. At that moment, however, so overcome with anger and disbelief, and a grief so deep and so extensive, he felt beyond any relief faith might bring.

His mother was the youngest of eight children and was always described by her brothers and sisters, her children and everyone who knew her, as a joyous, loving person. His mother loved to dance. His mother loved life. His mother lived for her family and was loved by them all. She and Donald were a truly loving, happy couple. Dennis knew calling his uncles would take every bit of strength and courage he could find within. He already knew it would be unbearable for them and for him.

Dennis said goodbye to his younger brother and promised to make the calls to his aunts and uncles right away. He also promised to make arrangements to bring his wife and children to their parents' home in Dunkirk, New York, the following day.

"Why did they take that tour," he thought. "Why them, God?"

Dennis walked over to the chair in the corner of the room, sat down and slowly dialed his uncle's number. Upon sharing the tragic news that his mother's body was still missing, Dennis broke down and sobbed.

***

As his brothers and friends were working on a plan to find the wreckage and victims, Bob had a difficult task of his own to complete. There had been some initial confusion about the identity of Mrs. Schrantz and Margarette de Munoz at the hospital. Mr. Schrantz and Margarette were rescued together. Mr. Schrantz had helped Margarette out of the airplane and stayed with her on his back the entire time in the water, since she couldn't swim. Mrs. Schrantz had also made it out of the plane but hadn't survived the icy water. It wasn't until the day after the accident that the survivors and victims who had been found and brought back the night before were all properly identified. The Jacobsen family had begun to work with the Alaska State Troopers, the coroner and the funeral home director to make arrangements to bring family members of survivors to Juneau and to send the victims bodies that had been recovered back to their homes.

The Schrantz family had all gathered at their parents' home in Dunkirk, New York, when they received a call they were waiting for.

"Hello, this is Bob Jacobsen, with Wings of Alaska in Juneau. Would Joe Schrantz be available?"

Joe's wife Liz had answered the phone. She held her hand over the receiver and announced to the room that there was a call from Alaska for Joe. The room - already filled with children and grandchildren - went completely silent.

Joe walked slowly to the phone, hoping and praying that whatever the news he got, he would be able to help his family members through their grief.

"Hello, Bob," he said, after taking the receiver from his wife's outstretched hand. "This is Joe."

"Joe, I wanted to let you know that we just got the go-ahead from the Alaska State Troopers. Your mother was found and we are going to be able to send both of your parents home. I am so sorry for your family's loss and what you're all going through."

Bob thought about how he and his own brothers and sisters would react to the death of both of their parents. Although they had all been together when their own father passed away two years before, Bob couldn't begin to imagine the grief the Schrantz family was feeling. Bob struggled to keep his feelings at bay while delivering this news. "I can only hope that you will find some comfort in knowing you can lay your parents to rest together," Bob said.

"Thank you, Bob, for letting us know. Can you please give me a minute to let my family know the news?"

"Of course," Bob said. "Be with your loved ones. We'll work with you and the funeral home here to take care of all the arrangements. You can call me or my sister Karen any time and we can help you facilitate whatever you need."

"Yes, thank you, Bob, we appreciate that. We'll be in touch."

Joe turned to the crowd already assembled in the living room, tears streaming down his face.

"That was the airline owner in Alaska," he said. "Mom and Dad will both be coming home."

Chapter Sixteen

June 24: Finding the Plane

June 23 was spectacular day in Juneau, just two days after the summer solstice and it would be daylight until midnight and dawn by 3 a.m. The weather was calm and clear and there wasn't a breath of wind when Jim Jacobsen took off in one of the Wings of Alaska deHavilland Beavers. The beauty of the snowcapped mountains and the shadows they cast was breathtaking. The sunshine reflecting off the water was a stark contrast to the grim task at hand and very dissimilar to the weather just 24-hours before. Jim could see the top of Mount Juneau, Gastineau Peak and the Devils Paw looking north into Canada.

Joining Jim in a second Beaver was Wings' pilot, Dave Fredericks, who knew Jim from their days working at Channel Flying in Juneau years before. Allen Shattuck flew on the plane with Dave to act as a spotter and to help with the search. They decided to fly out to the crash site and planned to fly in a grid pattern to look for any signs of the downed plane. Although the US Coast Guard had told Bob the plane was at a depth of 150 feet, they neglected to drop a buoy to mark its location.

Errol Champion had a hand-held VHF radio onboard his boat and was able to stay in contact with Jim and Dave flying above. Also searching that evening was Bill Corbus, in his 18-foot skiff with a 40-horse-power motor.

Errol and Bill had been going up the Taku River since the 1970s. Over the years, they had seen many areas where the ground fog obliterated the surface of the water. They knew the river well and were familiar with its many sand bars and tidal changes. Even though they had an idea of where to search for the plane, they knew the murky water's depths, the strength of the river current, glacial silt and big tides that time of year might still obscure the remains of the aircraft, even from the sonar.

Jim and Dave searched for slightly more than an hour when Dave spotted oil on the water. He had been flying at a higher altitude than Jim's plane and was able to direct Jim to the spot, aware what they were seeing was likely fuel from the plane.

"Errol, this is Jim," he radioed. "Dave and I can see what might be fuel coming to the surface. Let me talk you through to the coordinates." Jim directed Errol's boat to the location from the air and then landed the Beaver on the river. He wanted to be able to look at any sonar images Errol might be able to get of what lay below the surface. After Jim landed, Dave and Allen continued back to Juneau, hoping their efforts would lead to a successful recovery of the plane and any victims that might still be aboard.

Errol's boat wasn't far from the location Jim gave him when he received the radio call and it didn't take him long before he was able to maneuver his boat into position. As he passed over the spot where the oil was most visible on the water's surface, Errol and his son Evan watched as the outline of an image began to appear on the sonar.

"Could that be the fuselage of an Otter?" Evan asked.

"I think so," Errol replied. "And look, Evan. Doesn't that look like it's a wing?" Errol pointed to an image on the sonar screen.

"Let's go over these coordinates a few times to get a clearer picture," Evan said. "I think I can make out the outline of what looks like the Otter fuselage and possibly a wing."

"That's definitely it," Errol said. "Let's put down a buoy here and mark the spot. It appears to be at a depth of about 90 feet; that's a whole lot better than what the Coast Guard told Bob yesterday."

"I'm going to radio the coordinates back to Mitch Falk and John Jacobsen on the *Gumption* and then I suggest we head back into town," Errol said.

"Yah, it might be shallow enough for them to send divers down to hook it if they get lucky," Evan said. "That's definitely what's left of the plane."

"At least we can let Bob and the and the Wings crew know we found where it is," Errol said. "That's the first step. Now comes the hard part."

Mrs. Florence Schrantz at Taku Glacier Lodge with the Hole in the Wall Glacier in the background. (Photos courtesy of the Schrantz family, from a camera recovered at the scene of the accident and returned to them by the Alaska State Troopers.)

Mr. Donald Schrantz at Taku Glacier Lodge, with the Taku River in the background. (Photo courtesy of the Schrantz family.)

Chapter Seventeen

The Gumption

By the time Mitch Falk and his landing craft the *Gumption* made it to the recovery site, they already knew the plane was on the bottom of the river. Bob arranged to have two divers from Commercial Dive Services, Pete Lind and Dick Callahan, go out to the site with them. Once they arrived, Jim Jacobsen landed the Beaver and anchored it in a nearby cove. Jim then came aboard the *Gumption* and they all discussed the next plan of action.

"Maybe we can send the divers down and tie a rope to the engine or something secure and just winch it up," Mitch suggested.

"That might work," Jim said. "It's worth a try."

Mitch had brought aboard a one-inch thick nylon line. He carefully looked over the rope, assessing its strength. Everyone aboard the *Gumption* was focused on their ad-hoc tasks in preparation for the divers to enter the murky waters and strong current. Monitoring the divers' equipment and making sure they were safe was the top priority.

"There's not much visibility at all," Pete said, as he jumped from the boat and hit the river.

"Honestly, it looks like there's zero visibility, Pete," Dick said. "Remember, Pete. The most important thing here is for you to be safe. Don't try or do anything unless you're exactly sure where you are and what's around you."

***

Dick and Pete had been under the water for about 20 minutes when they came back up to the surface.

"We managed to tie the rope onto something," Dick said. "But honestly, there's a complete lack of visibility down there, there's cut up sheet metal, there's struts sticking up. I'm not sure if we got the line secured or not, but we can't do any more. It's just not safe for us to be down there. And we need to be really careful because we think the fuselage is sitting on a ridge. If the plane moves the wrong way, it will go deeper and we might not be able to reach it at all."

"You're right," Jim said. "We for sure don't want anyone else hurt. We can only try and do what we can and what's best. I don't think it's a good idea to dive on the Otter any more."

The men consulted and decided it would be best to wait for a slack tide before they tried to begin the winch process. Southeast Alaska experiences significant changes in the tides. There can be up to a 25-foot difference in the depth of the water depending on the moon; from a minus 4 to a plus 21-foot change can occur in about 6½ hours. It's extremely important for Alaska mariners to be aware of the tide changes and not fight the powerful currents.

"The current is swift in this area," Mitch said. "I think we all agree we should wait for the tide to go slack, right?"

There were nods in agreement all around. "OK then; let's all grab something to eat," Jim said. "This isn't easy work, folks. I need to keep my beautiful figure," he joked. John and Matt sat down in the galley of the *Gumption* while Mitch began to prepare a meal.

"Grab some coffee while you wait, guys." Mitch said. "Allen Shattuck is going to come out on the Reinell to help us again, so with the tides the way they are, it's going to be a few hours before we can do anything else."

***

Later, when Mitch thought it was safe to try again, the men slowly began the process of using the winch to raise the wreckage.

After a few minutes into the winching process Mitch yelled, "Stop! Damn it. I think we lost it," shaking his head and realizing the rope had become too slack.

"We had it," John said. "I can't believe we lost it."

"Look guys, it's late and we've been out here all day. I think we should head back into town and come back out tomorrow morning," Jim said quietly, sensing everyone's frustration. "We're all tired and it's been a really long day. We can come back out after we all get some good sleep."

"I think we might have lost the location too. It looks like the buoy marking the spot moved," Mitch said.

"I really think we should just head back to the dock and regroup," Jim said again.

"I'm sure Errol will be willing to come back out with the sonar and see how far off the marker the Otter has moved," John said. "We can think about getting some other boats out here too."

"You all did good work today," Jim added. "I know we're disappointed, but we can get it again. Tomorrow let's bring out our boat too, John, and we can meet at Bob's house tonight and come up with Plan B."

"It's already tomorrow," John said, looking at his watch. "I think you forgot you're in the land of the midnight sun, big brother."

Chapter Eighteen

Miguelito

Rosa Maria Gomar de Vides was examined by three doctors while at Bartlett Memorial Hospital. They all wanted to be sure they hadn't missed something in their exams. Rosa showed no signs of physical injuries from the accident. Despite symptoms of mild hypothermia when she was brought in, by the afternoon of June 23, the doctors all agreed that Rosa was physically well enough to be released the next day.

Rosa's older brother, Miguel Angel Gomar and his wife Susie, along with her older sister Haydee Gomar de Fernandez and her sister's husband Leonel Fernandez, took the first flight out of Guatemala City when they were notified by the Alaska State Troopers of their mother's death and told of Rosa and her children's status. Rosa's best friend, Gretchen Luttmann, also made plans to leave her home and family in Costa Rica to be at Rosa's side. They all arrived in Juneau the next day.

Wanda Gard's son Larry, who was traveling on business in Savannah, Georgia, also came to Juneau to help his mom and take her home. Doctors determined that Wanda should remain in the hospital a couple more days due to a possible heart problem caused by the hypothermia and issues with her blood sugar. The doctors found that Wanda had sustained injuries where the seat belt from the plane had bruised her internal organs and that she had severe bruising and an injury to a ligament in her leg.

The physicians also decided that 67-year old Margarette de Munoz would remain hospitalized under observation, as they were concerned about her heart and wanted to closely monitor her. Unfortunately none of Margarette's children could arrange to come to Juneau on short notice, but Miguel and Haydee considered their mother's friend as family and treated her as such during their Juneau stay and included her in their plans to return to Guatemala.

Unfortunately, Rosa's family support had not yet arrived when she was asked to complete an impossible task no parent should ever have to face.

Kieran O'Farrell was taking a short break from helping Wanda and was sitting in the Bartlett Hospital stairwell when she saw Rosa Maria coming up the stairs along with an Alaska State Trooper and a Bartlett nurse. Tears were visibly streaming down Rosa's face. The group was returning from the hospital morgue where Rosa had just identified her daughter Maria's body.

"I'm with Wings of Alaska," Kieran said, as Rosa passed her in the stairwell. "I cannot tell you how sorry I am for your incredible loss. If there is anything I can do, please don't hesitate to ask," Kieran said.

Rosa stopped walking for a moment. She looked directly at Kieran. "Take care of George," Rosa said softly.

Kieran was in disbelief. "Our company just killed your mother and children and you're telling me to take care of the pilot who was responsible for taking their lives," Kieran thought to herself.

As if she could feel what Kieran was thinking, Rosa continued softly. "God has a plan for our lives that we have not been given the blueprint to. My children are playing in fields with God right now."

Later that evening, recounting the experience to a few of her fellow Wings employees, Kieran was still in awe. "Prior to seeing Rosa early this morning, I had a definition of faith," Kieran said. "In that hospital stairwell, when things were the worst I could ever imagine and Rosa said that, I realized something. I realized that faith begins when understanding ends. I will never forget that moment or ever look at my problems or my life the same way again," Kieran said.

Kieran wasn't the only one awed by Rosa's strength. After being released from the hospital the next day and checking into a room at the Baranof Hotel, Rosa told her brother and sister that she wasn't leaving Juneau without her mother and Miguelito being found.

"We have to find them. We can't leave them here," she said. Her friend Gretchen sat down on the bed next to Rosa and took her hand in hers.

"Rosa, I spoke with the sister of the president of the company and she told me they are looking for the airplane," Gretchen said. "Your mother's body might be in the plane, but you told us little Miguelito floated away down the river."

Rosa sobbed, falling into her friend's arms. "We can't leave them here."

Miguel and Haydee spoke softly to each other as Gretchen comforted their sister. “Rosa,” Miguel said. “Maybe we can rent a helicopter or a plane and go look for him ourselves.”

Rosa looked up. “Yes, yes,” she said softly. “We have to look for him. He was wearing a red raincoat. Maybe he’s on the side of the river?” Rosa sobbed and everyone in the room felt the incredible weight of her sadness, along with their own.

“You rest now,” Haydee said. “Miguel and Leonel will go out and see how we can rent a plane or a helicopter.”

“I have to go with them to look for him,” Rosa said. “Promise me you won’t let them go without me.”

“Are you sure, Rosa?” Haydee asked, incredulous that Rosa would even consider getting back on a small plane or helicopter so soon after the accident.

“Promise me, Haydee,” Rosa said. "I have to go."

Miguel walked back to the edge of the bed where Rosa was sitting. He leaned down in front of her and took his sister’s face in his hands.

“I promise you,” he said. “If that’s what you want, Rosa, we’ll rent a helicopter and we will all go together tomorrow to look for Miguelito.”

Chapter Nineteen

Plan B

Mitch Falk woke up early on Saturday morning and decided to call his friend Scott McCallister to see if he could get two halibut anchors from him to take aboard the *Gumption* before they headed back to the accident site.

"I have this idea," Mitch said to the group that met on the dock in Juneau that morning to head up river. "Scott gave me these two halibut anchors and since it will take a couple hours to get to the site, I can try welding them together to make one large grappling hook." A single halibut anchor can weigh hundreds of pounds. Mitch thought that if he could weld two anchors together, it would make a better hook for snagging the downed plane.

"That's a great idea," John said. "You think you can do it on the boat?"

"Yah, it won't be easy to weld while we're moving and I know it's a long shot, but I think it's worth a try."

The Wings crew along with the *Gumption* would continue working together running boats and planes back and forth to the site trying to hook enough of the airplane's fuselage to bring the plane to the surface. High winds and high seas and a weather front moved in on Saturday hampering their efforts through Sunday.

Frustrated with the lack of progress, Mitch suggested that the Jacobsens hire Scott McCallister, and his 58-foot-limit seiner the *Owyhee,* and Wayne Alex, with his seiner the *Pacific Bell,* to assist with the recovery efforts. Wayne Alex was known throughout Southeast Alaska as as an expert logger, rigger, and fisherman. The *Owyhee* was equipped with the latest sonar technology – searchlight sonar – that could be used to help find the exact location the plane may have moved to when they lost it the night before. The *Owyhee's* sonar was able to transmit a cone of sound out at an angle and was capable of searching larger areas than the down-sounder sonar on Errol Champion's river boat that had been originally used to find the wreckage.

When Jim called to get the OK from Bob to contract with the *Owyhee* and the *Pacific Bell,* Bob was in his office. The brothers agreed more boats and more help at the recovery site were needed.

"Yah, It's such a slow process, Bob," Jim Jacobsen said.

"We hook the plane and tow it for a ways, then it comes loose. There's a river current and a tidal current sometimes flowing together and other times working against each other. Sometimes we get the plane flying along with us under water and one of the currents gets us and it drags a wing or something and we lose it."

"It's like going into a dark room with earplugs and trying to catch a fly with a fishhook - a big fishhook and a slow fly, maybe."

"You'll get it," Bob said. "If it can be done, you'll get it done."

Bob approved adding Scott and Wayne to the team. "Thanks for the update Jim. Keep me posted. We have to send those people home."

***

By Monday morning the weather had improved and the larger ad-hoc recovery group resumed the search.

"When you called me," Scott McAllister said,"my first thought was, 'Why the heck are you guys calling me. Why aren't the Coast Guard and the Troopers out there looking? They have all the experience and the equipment.'"

"Those were our thoughts exactly," Jim said. "None of us could believe the Coast Guard would give up searching less than 15 hours after the accident with four victims still missing. My brother Johnny here had a few choice words to say about how he felt hearing that news."

"I guess you do what you have to do," Scott said. "I just hope we can help."

"Our family appreciates your willingness to try," Jim said. "It really means a lot to all of us," he added, working to ignore the frustration and anger he had been feeling since he'd heard about the accident and the federal and state agencies pulling out of the search.

One of Scott's crew members, James Van Campen, interrupted the conversation to ask where Scott wanted him to put some supplies. The men quickly shifted into work mode, preparing for a long day on the river.

On Monday afternoon – almost a week after the accident had occurred – the recovery team finally had a breakthrough.

Wayne Alex dropped the homemade grappling hook on one side of his boat then circled around the area where they knew the downed plane had settled. He hoped the line would serve as a lasso and when the grappling hook finally hit the plane, he'd have the wreckage secure enough to be able to bring it to the surface. The rigging of the booms would handle the weight of the aircraft, but there was limited line capacity on the strongest boom winch, so the recovery would have to be done in a series of short lifts. There were also stability considerations. The plane's recovery would all have to be done with the full weight of the airplane hanging over the side of the boat, compromising its stability. Finally, there were the river currents to consider. The Alaska bore tides were huge at the time, running over 20-foot tidal differences, that would further complicate matters.

The entire operation would be dicey at best.

"It's sometimes better to be lucky than good," Scotty McAllister said to his crew, watching Wayne's maneuvers. "But Wayne has to be both good and lucky to pull this off."

As the others watched, Wayne's approach miraculously seemed to work.

The grappling hook hit the fuselage. Wayne used his winch to begin pulling what was left of the plane to the surface. Everyone still hoped, but no one knew for sure, that the missing victims were still inside.

Once again, Wayne's creativity and years of experience and expertise as a rigger came into play. The boat's deck winch alone didn't have the power to pull the plane to the surface. He devised an ingenious way to pull the rope up a little bit with the winch, wrap a chain strap around the line, put a hook in to secure it, then lift up the line a little more, winching and pulling bit-by-bit. Wayne repeated this maneuver a number of times until they could see the fuselage come up near the surface below and aft of *Pacific Bell's* stern.

The body of one of the victims who had been inside the wreckage of the Otter floated out and upward just as the plane neared the surface of the river. The divers Dick Callahan and Pete Lind saw the body, jumped in the river and recovered the victim, who was later determined to be 69-year old Caroline Garner, a passenger from Michigan.

While Pete and Dick focused on recovering the body, John Jacobsen and Matt Roys helped Wayne with the fuselage. Everyone was working efficiently and silently, as they faced the harsh reality of death. The men knew it was still unsafe for the divers to enter the Otter to see if other victims remained inside.

Scotty McAllister happened to look down the river as each man focused on his respective task. As they all knew, the tide changes around the solstice were some of the biggest of the year. Scott thought he could make out a huge wave of water moving toward them in a tidal surge.

In late June the glacial runoff into the Taku River is at the highest and June 27 just happened to be a day when the swing between the low and high tides on the river was also at its highest - close to 22 feet. The conditions caused a bore tide similar to the ones surfers like for catching a big wave. This tidal surge, however, would spell absolute disaster for the boats and the recovery efforts. If they lost the plane again or if the boats ended up being pushed by the tide up onto the mudflats, there would be no Plan C for recovering the wreckage or the bodies of the remaining victims.

All the men knew they would have to deal with the flood tide current, but Scotty never expected to see the large wall of water he saw coming directly toward them. He knew Wayne would have a problem keeping both his boat safe and the plane secure.

"Look," Scotty yelled to his crew and the men on the other boats, pointing toward the tidal surge they could make out slowly heading toward them. "This is a disaster."

The *Owyhee* crew leapt into action. Scotty maneuvered the *Owyhee* alongside the *Pacific Bell.* "Hey Wayne," he shouted, pointing to the surge coming toward them. "You've got to drop your anchor now. I need a man on the bow to receive a tow line. Shit's about to fly."

Wayne shouted to his crewman to go the bow. Scotty pulled the *Owyhee* forward and one of his crew threw over a line that was fastened to the *Pacific Bell's* bow cleat.

"I'm going to drop my anchor and put the boat in gear," Scotty yelled to the men aboard Wayne and Mitch's boats. "We'll keep pulling on you, Wayne, as that tidal surge comes in, to keep it from pushing you onto the flats."

As the force of the tide and the wall of water moved toward the boats, Scotty ran the *Owyhee's* engine at 1400 rpm, which normally would have put his speed at about eight knots moving forward. With his towline on the *Pacific Bell* and what was left of the Otter now flying behind it, the two boats and the airplane barely managed to remain in place.

Wayne was completely focused on keeping the rigging in place and his boat under control. Scotty focused on controlling their positions on the water.

The boats and the plane were strung out in a train; *Owyhee* with her anchor down, running against the tide, *Pacific Bell* with her anchor down, and the plane flying in the current, astern. All they could do was hang on until the tidal surge settled. It took more than three hours before the incoming current let go and the boats were safely out of the tides push.

"I've been a fisherman my whole life," Scotty said to his crew when the crisis had passed, "and I've fished from Mexico to the Bering Sea, but this was one of those times when we got really lucky and everything just went right. I thought for sure we were going to end up grounded on the mudflats in front of the Taku Glacier and lose the plane again."

The men sat quietly. They were grateful for their success as they contemplated what they knew could have been. Mitch Falk finally broke the silence.

"We're going to have to wait another few hours for high tide and then we can tow the wreckage into Sunny Cove, where the waters will be shallower. We can wait there until the tide goes out and we'll be better able to get inside to look for the other victims."

The men agreed that would be the safest plan. A few hours later the *Pacific Bell* and the *Gumption*, with its flat-bottom hull, motored slowly toward the shallower waters of Sunny Cove, just South of Annex Creek.

As the *Gumption* began its slow journey, Jim was able to contact Bob via marine radio with the news of their success.

"Bob, I've got some news," Jim relayed. "It's kind of a miracle actually. We were able to bring up the wreckage and recover the body of one of the victims at the site when we brought the plane near the surface. We're headed into Sunny Cove to get to shallower water before we go inside," Jim said. "Can you meet us out there with the Reinell and help us?"

"Oh my Lord, Jim. You did it," Bob said. "Thank you."

"It's been tough, brother. We'll talk more when you get here and I'll fill you in on what happened."

"Ok, thank everyone for me, will you?"

"Sure," Jim said. "And Bob, make sure you bring out another couple of body bags. We think the ones we had with us may have gone back to town on Scotty's boat. We may not have enough onboard if we find the other victims."

"OK, I'll see you in a couple hours," Bob radioed.

Bob looked at the clock in his office. It was close to 7 p.m. on June 27 and he was dealing with details for the memorial service set to take place the next day. He reached down to open a box he had set next to his desk, just in case. "More body bags," he thought. "Not something I ever imagined I'd be glad to have on hand from the Troopers."

Bob couldn't process the mix of thoughts and emotions swirling through his mind and body: relief for having fulfilled his promise to be able to send the bodies of the victims back to their families; sadness for the incredible loss and for not finding Miguel; rage at the authorities for giving up the search and recovery efforts so quickly; gratitude for his family, friends, employees and community for taking on the task; anger at George for his mistake that caused it all; anxiety and sadness for knowing the pain this accident caused. Mostly, Bob felt an overwhelming sense of guilt and responsibility that he knew he could never let go of.

"This is all my fault," he thought for the hundredth time since the accident occurred. "I was responsible for preventing it from happening in the first place. What more could I have done to make sure all my pilots had the judgment to avoid this accident?"

As he sat at his desk, one hand on the box of body bags, Bob knew he needed to let the Alaska State Troopers know the status of the recovery efforts and let the funeral home director know he'd need to be met at the dock when he returned. Then Bob turned his attention to what else he'd need aboard the Reinell in order to join his brothers and the remaining recovery team at Sunny Cove.

Bob contacted his two most senior maintenance technicians, Don Bach and Mike Thomas, and asked them to assist with the recovery of the Otter. Any time a plane crashes, the mechanics don't sleep well worrying if the accident was caused by a mechanical failure. Bob knew Don and Mike could be a big help getting the wreckage aboard the *Gumption*.

***

In the early morning hours on June 28, when the wreckage was finally grounded in Sunny Cove and the tide had gone out, Matt Roys, Don Bach, Mike Thomas, and John, Jim and Bob Jacobsen worked together to carefully carry the bodies of Kathleen Pruneski and Rosita Gomar de Vidas, Rosa's mother, out of the plane and onto the deck of the Bayliner.

"It's so strange," Matt said, looking down at the women as they worked to place one of the victims inside the body bag provided by the Troopers. "They look so normal." Because of the iciness of the water, the bodies were eerily preserved. Matt could see the brush strokes where one of the women had applied makeup to her face the morning of the accident. The putrid smell of death was everywhere.

"I don't think I'll ever forget this smell," John whispered to Matt as they zipped the bag around the woman and began to prepare another body bag for the second woman on board.

"Do you know who these people are?" Matt asked.

"I think the woman we found earlier who Bob is bringing back to Juneau on the Reinell is a woman from Michigan. I understand that there was some confusion with the Troopers identifying people at the hospital the night of the accident, but they know now," John said.

"John and Matt, you guys should head back to the fuel dock. We'll radio the Troopers and let them know you're on your way," Jim Jacobsen said.

"Why don't you head back now, John and Matt, and I'll be behind you after we make sure the Troopers and the funeral home van can meet you there," Bob said.

"The rest of us will stay out here and trim up the plane as best we can to lift it and fit it onto the deck of the *Gumption*. We'll need to be really careful with it because the NTSB will need it in their investigation."

The National Transportation Safety Board is responsible for investigating all airplane accidents, and the recovery of airplane parts can give important clues as to the causes of crashes.

"OK," John said. "I think we should be able to make it back to Juneau by about 5 a.m."

"Be careful," Jim said. "We're all pretty exhausted. Just be safe. You both did good. Those families will finally be able to have some closure."

"We're just trying to do what's right," Matt said. "I hadn't really thought much about what it will mean to them. Thanks for saying that, Jim. I'll be back some time tomorrow to help with the plane."

"I'm going to stay here a little longer and help get the plane loaded onto the *Gumption*," Bob said.

As the Bayliner slowly made its way down the river toward Juneau to bring the bodies of the final victims home, John was suddenly overcome with grief thinking about the last six days and the little boy Miguel that still hadn't been found. He had heard from his friends at ERA Helicopters that Rosa Maria's family had hired them to go out to look for little Miguel and knew that Bob had arranged to have the payment for their flights sent to him. Though they hadn't been successful in finding Miguelito, he knew Rosa would be relieved they were able to recover her mother's body.

Neither the Jacobsen brothers, nor any of the other men who participated in the recovery efforts, knew then that it would take a few weeks and some fairly heavy drinking for some of them to be able to sleep through the night. The same Alaska-tough, get-the-job-done attitude that allowed them to accomplish the mission the authorities had given up on, was what also prevented them from talking about or processing their own trauma and sadness.

***

When Bob arrived at the dock in the early morning, the Troopers and the funeral home director were already there waiting at the gate. He looked at his watch. It was 6:45 a.m. He knew it would be late enough in Michigan to place a phone call there. He reached into the vest pocket of his shirt and took out a small piece of paper with the names and phone numbers of each of the victim's families he had been keeping in touch with since the day after the accident.

He and his brothers had decided to bring the victims and the airplane wreckage back to the dock of Taku Oil Sales, the fuel company started by the Jacobsens' parents. The property and dock were located about a mile away from downtown Juneau, along a more private area than where the Wings planes started and ended their tours. Bob didn't want another family's grief to be compounded by a newspaper photo of their loved one in a body bag or on a stretcher, like the photo the Schrantz family had to endure from the night of the accident. Bob was still upset that the newspaper photographer had taken pictures of the survivors being put into ambulances when they were first brought back to Juneau.

Bob walked slowly from the dock into the Taku Oil Sales office building. He had already spoken to one of Caroline Garner's two sons, John and Alan, to express his sympathies and to keep them updated on the plans to find and recover the plane and their mother's body. Now, he knew, he'd finally be able to tell them that their mother was found.

"Get yourself together," he thought to himself as he fumbled in his jacket pocket for the key to get into the building to make the phone call. "Get yourself together. I need to let John and Alan know their mom is coming home."

Chapter Twenty

The Church Service

Bob was getting ready to attend the Catholic Church mass in Spanish that Karen had arranged for Rosa, along with her family and friends who had flown to Juneau to help her after the accident. He knew they had been going out almost every day to search for Miguel and though they had not found any signs, the family still hoped they would be able to bring all their family members back to Guatemala for burial. They appreciated the memorial service Karen had arranged and were grateful that their mother's remains had been found and brought back to Juneau that morning.

As Bob dressed for the service, his thoughts went to the hospital visit he had with George Coulter the morning after the accident.

When they had met with Catholic Bishop Michael Kenny to plan the church service, Bishop Kenny had spoken to the Jacobsen family about God's love and God's forgiveness. That morning, however, as he tried to find the strength to carry on, Bob still felt angry with George for his mistake. The person he was most angry with, however, was himself.

"I screwed up, Bob," George had said to him in the hospital during Bob's visit the morning after the accident.

"Yes, you did, George," Bob said. "But I heard about what you did to help save people and I'm really glad you made it through."

"When I was in the water and I thought for sure I was going to die," George said, "I just wanted the chance to tell everyone I was sorry. I just wanted to tell Rusty and Mike I was sorry that I didn't listen to them when they said the weather was better on the east side. I should have crossed over sooner. I just wanted to tell them how sorry I am."

"I'm glad you'll have the chance now, George," Bob had said. "Just get well. We'll talk more later. Just get well, OK."

When Bob left George's room that morning, he had gone on to visit Rosa and the other survivors, Wanda Gard and Margarette de Munoz. On this evening, however, Bob was still searching for compassion for George, even if he couldn't find forgiveness. It was George who had taught Bob how to fly in Oregon when he was a student at the University of Oregon. Bob was the one who asked George to come to Juneau when he and Drew first started Wings of Alaska 12 years earlier.

Bob knew in his heart that Wings had outgrown George's management abilities. That's why he had made the decision to change the management structure and take the Chief Pilot responsibilities away from George. "I didn't handle it well when I put Rusty and Mike in charge," Bob thought. "I could have done a better job of telling George why we needed to make the change and I could have done better at dealing with all the egos and personalities involved."

"Could I have prevented this?" he thought. "I'm the President of Wings of Alaska. I'm the guy in charge. I'm the one who is responsible for all of this. It's my fault those children are dead," he said to himself.

Every time Bob thought about Rosa and the children, he felt both overwhelming guilt and great gratitude that his own sons were healthy and he could still tuck them into bed at night. The sound of someone coming up the stairs brought him back into the present. Bob heard a knock at the door.

Karen came into the bedroom to check to see if Bob was ready for the memorial service. "We should leave in 15 minutes, Bob," she said. "Are you almost ready?"

"I don't know if ready is the right word," Bob said.

"I know how you feel," Karen replied.

What Bob later wished he had said right then to his older sister was, "Thank you, Karen, for all you have done in response to this awful tragedy and for always standing by me and protecting our family and our company, no matter what. You are an amazing woman, Karen, and I love you."

But Bob wasn't yet that kind of man. Instead he added to his long list of regrets. He just shook his head slowly and said, "No, Karen. I'm not sure you do. I'm really not sure you do."

***

The Jacobsen family all loved Bishop Michael Kenny. Their company had flown him all around Southeast Alaska for years while he traveled in his capacity as a leader of the Catholic Church. In addition to being their Bishop, they considered him a family friend. Karen had always called him "Wings favorite passenger." When their business was just getting started, the Bishop had starred in a comical television commercial for Wings showing him running through the airport to get on a Wings of Alaska plane saying, "Heaven can wait, but Wings can't."

Bishop Kenny had been out of town the night the accident occurred, but as soon as he came back to Juneau he immediately headed for the Wings of Alaska office to offer help.

"I'd love it if you could visit the two women from Guatemala and their family members who just arrived," Karen had said.

Not only did Bishop Kenny visit the family, he arranged to do an entire mass in Spanish at the Cathedral of the Nativity of the Blessed Virgin Mary, the church for the Diocese of Juneau that covers all of Southeast Alaska from Yakutat to Ketchikan, all along the Canadian border.

The small beautiful Cathedral where all the Jacobsen children had been confirmed was already full of longtime friends and employees by the time the Gomar de Vides family arrived to take their seats in the front pews.

Two beautiful bouquets of fresh Alaska flowers stood in vases at the front of the altar. Karen thought that the out-stretched arms of Jesus on the cross at the front of the Church felt welcoming. The statue of the Virgin Mary behind the altar looked especially sad to her.

"We're here today to honor the lives of Rosita Maria Gomar and her beautiful grandchildren Miguel Gomar de Vidas and Maria Gomar de Vidas," Bishop Kenny said. "It's hard when we lose anyone we love unexpectedly and we all know it is especially hard when children are taken from us."

"Let me remind you, please, that we are all children of God. I know He is welcoming all of His children with open arms into their eternal home with Him."

The organ music began to play.

"Let us pray," he said.

Chapter Twenty-One

Returning Home

Rosa, Margarette and Rosa's family flew back to Guatemala the day after the church service, along with Rosita and Maria's remains. Despite Rosa's resolve and everyone's best efforts, Miguelito's remains were not with them.

Upon their arrival in Guatemala City, both Haydee and Miguel offered to bring Rosa to their homes. Neither wanted her to go back to the house she had only months before shared with her husband Byron Vides and only weeks before was a home filled with children's laughter. Byron, an economist, met them at the airport and offered to return with Rosa to their home. He knew how much Rosa loved the log home they had designed and built together and moved into as a family in 1991. He also knew how difficult it would be for her to return there alone.

Rosa and Byron had separated just months before the Alaska trip, originally planned as a family vacation. When he and Rosa separated, Byron hadn't wanted her to take the children without him, but eventually changed his mind when Rosita and Margarette decided to travel in his place. Whether out of love, grief or guilt, or a combination of them all, Byron still hoped he and Rosa might fix their marriage and get back together. As he sat in the airport waiting for the plane to arrive, Byron's thoughts momentarily turned to the fun he and Rosa had designing their log home and to the good times they had there together as a couple and a family. Simultaneously he was filled with an equal dose of guilt and anger, but he knew Rosa needed support through the impossible transition of returning to her home alone.

Rosa, however, knew in her heart that if she didn't go directly home after she left the airport it would be much harder for her to do the next day. Overriding Byron's misgivings and the objections of her brother and sister, Rosa went home from the airport, walking into the house that was so familiar and yet, at the same time, so unrecognizable. When everyone finally left, Rosa walked through the silent hallway into her children's rooms. Seeing Miguelito's bed, she finally broke down and sobbed.

***

Wanda Gard was grateful Kathleen Pruneski's remains had been found and that she was returning home. Since she and Kathy were not a married couple, however, Kathleen's parents' legal rights as her next of kin superseded what Wanda wanted as Kathleen's final resting place. Kathleen was ultimately buried according to her parents' wishes. Wanda's family and friends surrounded her throughout those difficult days, doing the best they could to offer their love and support. They encouraged Wanda to continue to focus on her physical healing as well as the emotional and spiritual steps needed to heal her grief.

The homecoming of Donald and Florence Schrantz and Caroline Garner's remains were also met by their families with a mix of grief and gratitude: overwhelming sadness at their loss and gratitude that their families could bury their loved-ones' remains. The days after the return to their homes were busy with preparations for funerals and remembrances. So too began each individual family member's process of picking up the pieces of their shattered life and moving forward in a world without their loved ones. And in the midst of it all, began the painful but inevitable legal process of placing a financial value on the lives that were lost.

Chapter Twenty-Two

The FAA Interview

The Juneau Federal Aviation Administration building was within walking distance of the Wings of Alaska hangar. Since its beginnings, Wings had a close working relationship with the FAA, collaborating on safety and noise issues relative to Juneau's air transportation community. Wings of Alaska prided itself on its safe flying record, coupled with its substantial growth in the market, while being a leader in aviation, business, and the Juneau community.

When Bob Jacobsen, Rusty Shaub, and Mike Stedman were asked to meet with the FAA's principal operations inspector Robert Kolvig on the morning of July 6th to discuss the accident, they went into the meeting without an attorney and with the intention to fully cooperate in every way possible with the on-going investigation. They had nothing to hide. All of the pilots had already individually provided their own written statements to the National Transportation Safety Board investigators describing what occurred the night of the accident. Even George Coulter was able to provide a statement from his hospital bed with details of what he remembered leading up to the accident.

When they entered the break room at the FAA's Juneau facility, no one from Wings of Alaska was prepared for the reception they were about to receive from the FAA staff.

"Good morning," said Kolvig, investigator for the FAA. Robert Kolvig had moved to Juneau from the East Coast. He'd previously served in the military, worked in law enforcement and had been an FAA investigator in Juneau for a number of years. As part of his duties Kolvig oversaw Wings of Alaska's participation in the FAA's Partnership for Safety Program under his jurisdiction. He was of medium height, stocky and slightly balding. There was nothing about Robert Kolvig that particularly stood out as unusual to any of the Wings employees who had gone with him on their required check rides or worked with him on aviation safety issues. That impression was about to change drastically.

"If you'll all take a seat, we'll get right into the interview. "Rusty, if you don't mind sitting directly across from me, I'd like to interview you about the night of June 22nd. We're going to be taping this and we'll be able to get a better recording," Kolvig said.

"No problem," Rusty said. Bob took a seat on one side of Rusty and Mike Stedman sat on the other. The FAA personnel sat directly across from them at the table. Kolvig turned on two tape recorders sitting in front of him and began.

"Ok, we are at the Juneau FAA Flight Standards District Office, in the break room of FSDO 5," he said. "The time is 8:03 in the morning and the date is July 6, 1994. We're here to talk with Rusty Shaub, Director of Operations for Wings of Alaska. Present also is myself, Robert Kolvig, Inspector with the FAA FSDO 5 Juneau; Ron Crumbaker, the Manager of FSDO 5 Juneau; Mr. Bob Jacobsen, President of Wings of Alaska; and Mr. Mike Steadman, Chief Pilot for Wings of Alaska."

"And it's our understanding that we are taping this conversation and that there are no objections. You will be provided, immediately following the interview, not only a copy, but an original, since we have two recordings going at the same time. Rusty, before we get started, I have a statement here that was signed by you; however, it says it's to the NTSB. I asked for a statement, is it also meant for me?" Kolvig asked.

"Sure," Rusty replied.

"Would you do me a favor so that there's no misunderstanding; would you just cross out NTSB and put FAA on the top and initial that please." Rusty reached across the table for the paper Kolvig had in front of him to make the requested change to the copy of his NTSB statement.

Bob had a sinking feeling when Kolvig asked Rusty to cross out NTSB and write FAA on his statement. He couldn't remember for sure, but he thought that what pilots shared with the National Transportation Safety Board as part of its work to determine the cause of an accident was confidential and could not be used in an enforcement proceeding by the FAA against the pilots who were helping the NTSB determine the cause. Though he knew all the pilots had independently shared their recollections of events leading up to the accident, something about the look on Kolvig's face when Rusty handed him back the initialed change made Bob uncomfortable. Bob wasn't sure why Kolvig already had a copy of Rusty's statement to the NTSB or how he had received it.

"Okay, thanks. Appreciate it," Kolvig said, looking quite pleased. "Alright, we'll go ahead and get started. I've just got some questions and I'll take you through it, Rusty. Just answer them to the best of your ability, the best of your knowledge, and just go from there. You can stop at any time if you want to take a break."

"Thanks," Rusty said.

"Alright, we're talking about June 22nd, of course, the date of the accident involving Nl3GA, George Coulter. And I understand that you were flying that day," said Kolvig.

"Yes, I was flying."

"Alright. Would you just generally describe what happened? Why don't you start at flying that day and generally what the weather conditions were throughout the day in the area."

"Well, the weather was generally good," Rusty said. "There were a few scattered areas. My first trip was at 10 in the morning I believe, to the lodge, and I was flying an Otter. We had cancelled the first trip of the day, which we frequently do, due to poor weather. But after 10 a.m. there were widely scattered areas of high clouds, I would say, 700- to 800- to l000-feet scattered. Then above that it was like 2500 to 3000 feet, broken as I recall, with patches of blue sky and occasional light rain showers. And that kind of weather continued on throughout the day. The scattered clouds and light rain would move around some, but in general, the ice cap planes were flying up the Taku River over the top of the Hole-in-the-Wall Glacier, you need at least 2500- to 4000-foot-ceilings to do that. And, as I recall, the weather stayed that way the whole day. The accident happened on the last trip of the day. When we got to the lodge it was raining lightly with ceilings about 1000-1500 broken and with five- to- six-miles visibility."

"Ok, so you got started at 10 a.m.?" Kolvig asked.

"Yes, that's right," Rusty answered, looking a bit confused. He had already answered that question.

"Alright," Kolvig replied. "Were there any delays at all, that morning?"

"Yes, as I already mentioned, the first flight of the day was cancelled. We had an 8 a.m. lodge trip that was planned, but it was canceled because of weather. One of the line pilots had gone up there to check. He couldn't get by the Taku Glacier so he returned and said we should cancel, so I remember we canceled the 8 o'clock tour."

Wings of Alaska would frequently have the new-hire line pilots do the weather checks because if they weren't comfortable with the weather, the flights would be cancelled.

"Who was the pilot that went up there earlier," Kolvig asked.

"I'm sorry I don't remember. I don't know. We have over two dozen pilots and I don't recall who was doing the weather check that morning."

"Getting to the flight itself, how long before the last flight from the lodge to Juneau - immediately preceding that flight back - before the accident occurred?" Kolvig asked.

"What flight are you talking about, Bob?" Bob Jacobsen interrupted. "I'm not sure I understand your question. Could you repeat your question so we could all understand it?"

"I'm talking about the flight when the accident occurred," Kolvig replied.

"Well, I don't recall exactly when we left," Rusty said. " We normally leave at 4:30 from the lodge back to Juneau and we are there by 5 o'clock. Wait, is that right?" Rusty asked, looking at Bob and Mike.

"It's usually about 5:30 back up from Juneau," Bob said. He could tell Rusty was nervous and uncomfortable with the line of questioning. Bob was concerned that Rusty wasn't fully back to himself after his own trauma of the accident and his rescue of two passengers and Kolvig's questions weren't clear. From his increasingly antagonistic tone and demeanor though, Bob was beginning to wonder if voluntarily sitting down with the FAA without an attorney was a good idea.

"Alright, and on that flight to the lodge," Kolvig asked, "can you tell me what kind of weather you encountered on that flight?"

"I've thought about it, a lot," Rusty said. "I remember thinking that there wasn't anything in particular that stood out as bad weather. There was a little weather right in the area by Annex Creek, as I recall, but it was, you know, it was, it was nothing bad. There was some heavy drizzle hanging around, I guess. That was about it. The visibility, going up the river, and the weather had improved to maybe 3000 feet broken at the lodge and 20 miles of visibility. The only hint of concerning weather was right in that Annex Creek area."

Bob was starting to feel in his gut that Kolvig might be leading Rusty toward a conclusion about the accident's cause that he may already have established in his own mind. It felt like Kolvig was looking to blame someone and he somehow had Rusty in his crosshairs, though neither Bob, Rusty or Mike could understand why. His concerns were confirmed and his thoughts were jolted back into the present by Kolvig's next question.

"Did Mike Olsen ever mention any kind of an altitude at all, did you ever hear him say anything about altitude?" Kolvig asked.

"No, I don't recall hearing anything," Rusty answered.

"He didn't say anything about an altitude? I'll go ahead and read you his statement here."

Kolvig read Mike Olsen's statement aloud, focusing on Mike saying that he had radioed back to the other four airplanes on the return trip from the Lodge that they may need to land due to low ceilings. FAA regulations state that pilots can go below 500 feet if they are setting up to land, but they aren't allowed to go below that minimum for any other reason.

"What he said, and I quote," Kolvig said, "was 'At this time there were fog layers between Flat Point, Jaw Point and Annex Creek. I started slowing down to prepare for landing. At that time, I was at 500 feet and descending between Flat Point, Turner Lake and Jaw Point. When I was at 100 feet and I could pick up shoreline at Jaw Point and Cooper Ridge, I aborted the landing and started climbing for Jaw Point and Cooper Ridge. I radioed back to the other airplanes that the visibility was good and they should all cross to the other side of the river. I received confirmation of my report from 36AK, Rusty Shaub." Kolvig put down Olsen's statement and looked directly at Rusty.

"Did he say he was at 100 feet?" Kolvig asked.

"Not that I recall," Rusty said. "He was out in front of me. I don't recall him ever saying that on the radio."

Kolvig was increasingly becoming more antagonistic. He raised his voice and stared straight at Rusty. "Turn and head to Jaw Point. And we may need to land due to low ceilings. Wasn't that significant to you at all?"

"Look, we fly float planes," Rusty said. "If we have a concern about weather, we set up to land on the river, or wherever we are in Southeast Alaska, and we wait it out. All these inland waterways are our runways and it's a safe alternative. That's the safest thing to do. If you have to land out there - if the visibility is low and you have to make a landing - you set up and you descend gradually to land. If you decide to land, of course you're going to get to 100 feet first before you land on the river. Mike and I both set up to land, but then Mike saw where it was clear and radioed back for everyone to cross to the other side of the river where visibility was good. I had already started to descend to land when he radioed that."

"Okay." Kolvig replied. "Well, I'm sure you know the regulatory requirements as far as altitude."

"Yes, of course," Rusty replied.

"And they're a minimum of what?"

"500 feet," Rusty said.

"Alright, now, there must have been some reason to descend from 500 feet to 200 feet. Either it was the visibility or it was the low ceiling, or a combination of both."

Bob Jacobsen again interrupted the interview in progress. "I think he answered you about this a couple of times already. He was setting up to land. He said the same thing in his written statement. It seems like you're trying to put words in his mouth."

"I'm not trying to put words in anybody's mouth, I'm just asking why he descended," Kolvig said.

"As I said, I think he answered that at least twice already," Bob Jacobsen said. "There was about three- maybe four - miles of visibility between Flat Point and the Turner River beach. An Otter is a big plane. As a pilot, I can tell you that you want to give yourself plenty of room to land straight ahead and that's what he was doing," Bob added, showing his frustration.

"Alright, is it common practice for you, every time you come down the river here, to descend to 200 feet in case you have to make a landing? Isn't that flying too low? Why didn't you just turn around and go back up to the lodge?"

"I probably could have done that," Rusty said. "But as I was setting up to land, Mike Olsen radioed that he had good weather near Turner Lake ahead of me on the river and we could just go across."

"When you descended to 200 feet and you were preparing to make a landing, did you radio back to the other aircraft?"

"I don't recall," Rusty replied.

"You are Director of Operations. Duties and responsibilities?"

"I'm a safety officer," Rusty replied. "I'm responsible for the safety and welfare of our pilots, passengers, airplanes."

"But you didn't make any calls, even though you were having to descend to land, you didn't tell anybody else in your flight behind you of the conditions you were encountering?"

"I was flying my airplane that night as a line pilot. We're a team up there. A call had already been made to all of us about the weather conditions by Mike Olsen, who was in the lead. The way things work, we follow our lead pilot. Nothing should have gone wrong that night. The weather wasn't that bad." Rusty said, looking down at his hands.

"So, even though you were preparing to land out there because of the conditions, you did not call back and tell the other aircraft. You didn't think that was important enough to call."

"I just hate it that you keep trying to put words in his mouth, Kolvig. I don't think that's appropriate," Bob Jacobsen said.

"Why didn't you call back to the other aircraft, Rusty?"

"Well," Rusty said quietly. "The line pilots had already been told where the concerning weather was and what to do to avoid it. Everyone who followed Mike's lead, including me, got back to Juneau and landed safely without a problem. None of us believed there should have been a problem. We never flew in conditions contrary to the Federal Aviation Regulations."

"How many more questions have you got, Kolvig?" Bob Jacobsen asked. "I think this might be a good place to take a break."

"Alright. Sure, we can take a break," Kolvig said. "The time is 8:31," he said, before turning off the tape recorders.

***

Bob, Rusty and Mike got up from the table and walked together out into the hallway of the FAA Building. "This interview is over," Bob whispered to Rusty. "This feels like a set up. They're not here looking for the truth about what happened. They've already made up their minds and have decided they're coming after us."

"It sure feels that way," Rusty said. "I feel like he's attacking me every time I say anything."

"He is definitely on the attack," Bob said. "Rusty, why don't you and Mike head back to the airport. I'm going back to the office. We're going to need more help."

"Ok, Bob," Rusty said. He looked more dejected than Bob had ever seen him. "I'll see you later."

"Hey, Rusty," Bob said, as Rusty began walking away with his head down and as if he had just been hit with a whip. "You didn't do anything wrong. You guys all avoided the bad weather. Don't let that F-ing Kolvig get to you. You put your life at risk to save others. You found survivors and you saved lives. You told the truth about what happened, Rusty," Bob said. "Everyone did. That's all we can do. It's absolutely legitimate to go below 500 feet to land on the river. As soon as you realized the ceilings and visibility were good near Turner Lake you aborted the landing and flew safely back to Juneau, just like you were supposed to do, and just like all the pilots did, except George."

"Thanks Bob." Rusty said, looking directly at Bob. "Kolvig sure as hell doesn't believe that. I thought he was supposed to be investigating the accident to find the cause."

"So did I, Rusty," Bob added. "So did I."

Chapter Twenty-Three

Legal Battles Begin

Allen Shattuck had been Bob's insurance broker for 10 years and their families had known each other since Bob was a child. The Shattuck family history in Juneau went back to the 1800s and their company, Shattuck and Grummett Insurance, was the first and the oldest insurance agency in Alaska.

After the accident, Allen Shattuck was one of the first people to reach out to extend his condolences and to offer help. He dropped everything to help, spending three days on the river searching for the victims and the airplane. His office had already worked with Wings of Alaska to help make arrangements for family members of survivors to come to Juneau. Allen exemplified the spirit of the Juneau community, where friends, neighbors and even strangers come together to help each other in times of need.

Within minutes of coming back to his office at the Wings of Alaska hangar after the meeting with the FAA, Bob picked up the phone and called Allen.

"Hi Allen. It's Bob again. Sorry you have to start your day talking to me."

"How you doing, buddy?" Allen asked.

"Not so good this morning actually. Rusty, Mike and I just met with the FAA," Bob said. "It was just a horrible meeting. We've been their 'golden boy' of safety in Southeast for years. You know we've been working so hard to raise the bar and improve safety for all the air carriers around here, but it seems that's all out the window now."

Allen interrupted. "You and your team have been leaders in all that, Bob," he said.

"Well, we went into that meeting without an attorney this morning intending to fully cooperate and to answer any questions they had. I think it was a big mistake. When they started questioning Rusty, their investigator, Kolvig, was insinuating Rusty and the other pilots were flying in bad weather and below FAA minimums. Allen, that just isn't true. Their line of questioning also centered on Rusty's role as the Director of Operations not following FAA mandated flight rules. I stopped the meeting after 30 minutes and just got Rusty out of there. It was a shock, Allen. I think we need an attorney familiar with the FAA to defend Rusty and the other pilots. Heck, we probably need someone to defend all of us if the FAA's going where I think they are."

"Bob, let me give you a name," Allen said. "You are going to need a good aviation attorney to help you. I met a man who gave a presentation at an insurance conference I went to that I was really impressed with. His name is Tim Miller. I saved his card. Hang on a second while I find his business card. I know I saved it."

Bob waited. He could hear Allen rummaging through his desk drawers.

"Here it is," Allen said. "He's with a big Oregon law firm, Martin, Bischoff, Templeton, Langslet & Hoffman, and he specializes in aviation issues. I suggest you give him a call. I'm so sorry you're going through this, along with everything else." Allen added. "The FAA is always looking for someone to blame. You know the saying, 'The FAA regulations are all written in blood.' People died, Bob, and with the FAA, it can't just be because it was an accident. Give this attorney Tim Miller a call and see what you think about him."

Allen had been one of the past owners of Southeast Skyways, the air carrier from which Wings of Alaska's original operating certificate had been purchased. He understood not only the insurance side of the aviation business, but also the regulatory and operational sides. Bob appreciated his knowledge and experience.

"I will, Allen. Thank you so much. And thanks for all you did to help get the family members of the passengers up to Juneau so quickly. The two women from Guatemala and the elderly woman from Michigan really needed support." Bob's voice trailed off. His visits with them and with George Coulter at the hospital were still just too raw to talk about.

"I know you're feeling all alone in all this, and I'm here to help all the way through this, any time of the day or night. You know you can call me."

"I can't tell you what that means," Bob said. "Thank you. I'll give Tim Miller a call right away. So long, Allen."

Bob looked at the notepad where he'd written down the name of the attorney. "Tim Miller, aviation attorney," he read. "I can sure use your help." He picked up the phone again and dialed the number and was pleasantly surprised when Mr. Miller's secretary put him through right away.

"Mr. Miller," Bob said. "My name is Bob Jacobsen and I'm the president of Wings of Alaska in Juneau, Alaska. You might have heard that our company had an accident with fatalities. I got your name from Allen Shattuck, who met you at an aviation insurance conference a few years ago."

"Yes," Tim said. "I read about your accident in the newspaper. I'm so sorry."

"Thank you," Bob said.

"Yes, I remember Allen. A nice guy," Tim added.

"He's been very helpful to us. Allen was impressed with you and thought you might be able to lend us a hand. We had a meeting with the FAA today that didn't go well. We met with them voluntarily and from their line of questioning it seemed to me they made up their minds that the other pilots, besides the accident pilot, were flying below FAA minimums. We haven't gotten anything official from them, but I think I made a mistake letting our Director of Operations, who was one of the pilots flying the line that night, sit down with the FAA investigator."

"Hey, don't tell me any more of the details right now," Tim said. "I'm looking at my calendar. I'm going to have my office reschedule everything and I'll be on a flight out of Portland to Juneau tonight. Can you arrange a hotel for me there and FAX me the details, along with your office address?"

"Yes, of course," Bob said. "Better yet, let me know what flight you get on and I'll pick you up at the airport. I have a feeling we'll be spending considerable time together."

"Look, this is a very important time for your pilots and your company. I'll come up for a day or two on my own dime and get an idea of what you need and you can see if we are the right fit for you. We can talk details when I get there and go from there."

"That's great," Bob said. "I'll FAX you some pertinent information and see you tonight." Bob put the phone down and could feel himself start to relax for the first time since leaving the FAA offices. "I hope this guy is as good a lawyer as Allen thinks he is," Bob said aloud, "because we sure can use some help."

Chapter Twenty-Four

Encouragement

Bob walked around his office pretending to look at the artwork on the wall. He tried to stop beating himself up for allowing Rusty to meet with the FAA. There were piles of phone messages to answer, stacks of letters and papers to read, checks to sign, a to-do list that was pages long, and a young family he hadn't seen in days. He desperately wished he could just leave it all behind, yet another light on his ever-ringing telephone was flashing. He almost didn't answer, though he knew there was no escaping what needed to be done.

"Hi Bob," he heard a friendly voice say. "It's Kirk Thomas in Ketchikan." Kirk Thomas and his family had owned and operated Tyee Airlines based in the Southern part of Southeast Alaska. They also operated successful fishing lodges in the region, including The Cedars Lodge in Ketchikan.

"Hello, Kirk," Bob replied. "It's great to hear a friendly voice. How are you?"

"Well," Kirk asked. "The question is, how are you?"

"I suggest we not go there, Kirk. Let's just say it's been rough lately," Bob said. "I'm sure you know about our accident."

"Actually, Bob, that's why I'm calling. You're not alone. There have been others of us that have experienced the path you are on. Mike Salazar, Jerry Scudero and I were talking about what you guys are dealing with up there. The three of us have been in your shoes. You need to know you'll pull through. You'll figure this out. You know, I was the sole owner of Tyee Airlines when we had accidents in 1979 and 1982. Thirteen people lost their lives. And I was the manager of Rocky Mountain Helicopters when that ship went down in Hobart Bay. I know you're familiar with that one. The accidents and the loss of life still haunt me to this day. Mike and Jerry have both had their tragedies too. There is no way anyone can know what you feel until they've stood in your shoes and God willing, few people will ever have the experience you and I have had of pulling dead bodies from the wreckage of an airplane."

Kirk paused for a moment and listened to Bob taking a few deep breaths.

"Bob," Kirk continued, "you'll be put to the test in the upcoming months and years as the FAA, the press and the attorneys for the deceased descend on you trying to discredit you as an individual, your family, your employees and your company. This accident will bring out the absolute worst in some people and fortunately the very best in others."

"I'm seeing that already," Bob replied.

"Bob, I just want you to know I think you guys have done a great job in aviation. I've respected you for a lot of years and I've followed your progress with great interest. I've ridden on your aircraft many times and have always been impressed with your service. Heck, I've even required my employees, including my own son, to use Wings of Alaska exclusively. I want you to know that my feelings about Wings haven't been altered one bit by this accident."

Kirk waited a minute in silence before Bob could reply.

"I can't begin to tell you how much your words mean to me right now, Kirk. We're all feeling pretty beat up. We were fortunate to recover three of the four victims' bodies recently and we're all trying to move forward as best we can. Unfortunately, Rusty, Mike Stedman and I just sat through an interview with that two-faced FAA jerk Kolvig. What a mistake that was."

"Oh, Bob. I'm so sorry. Mike, Jerry and I have all heard down here in Ketchikan that the FAA is out to make an example of you," Kirk said. "When I say, I understand, I do, Bob. You need to find a good attorney."

"Thanks for that advice and thanks for mentioning Mike and Jerry," Bob said. I've got great respect for you Ketchikan guys. The flying weather in southern Southeast is more challenging than we have up here."

"I know how easy it would be for you to quit right now but the loss would be an another tragedy," Kirk added.

Bob felt as if God had reached down and allowed Kirk to say the exact words he needed to hear. "Thank you for sharing your experience and words of encouragement," Bob said.

"I won't take any more of your time," Kirk said. "When you come to Ketchikan please come see us at The Cedars. You are welcome any time and bring Darlene. I can show you some great fishing."

"I'm not much of a fisherman, Kirk, but I sure appreciate the offer. Of course the same goes for you when you're in Juneau," Bob said, "although I'm not sure what I can offer. I'll always be indebted to you."

"Just keep doing what you're good at, Bob. Let's stay in touch and let me know if there's anything I can do."

After Bob said goodbye and hung up the receiver, he looked back at the piles on his desk once again. Somehow, in that moment, everything there was to do seemed less daunting.

Chapter Twenty-Five

John and "The Bobs" Go to Bat

John Litten was a funeral home director, the longtime manager of Sitka Tours, a respected leader in the Alaska visitor industry and former president of the Alaska Visitors Association, a mentor to Bob Jacobsen, and friend of Holland America's CEO Kirk Lanterman.

John had a relationship with Holland America Line that preceded the tenure of Kirk Lanterman as CEO. He helped the company when there was a fire aboard its cruise ship, *Prinsendam,* in the Gulf of Alaska in 1980. While all of the ship's passengers and crew were safely rescued, passengers were taken to Sitka and Valdez aboard the oil tanker *Williamsburg* and the Coast Guard Cutter *Boutwell* to await being able to return home. It was the most successful passenger rescue effort ever undertaken by the Coast Guard.

When John got a call for help from Holland America, which at the time didn't have any employees stationed in Sitka, he spearheaded a community-wide effort to open up the town to the stranded passengers, making sure they had clothing, food, lodging and medications, and anything else the town could provide while passengers waited up to a week to be able to return home. His efforts on behalf of Holland America Line earned him the gratitude of the cruise line and the respect of its soon-to-be, notoriously tough CEO Lanterman, who was rising in the ranks of the company at the time.

"He was a wonderful person, as long as you never worked for him," John once said of Lanterman. "His demands were relentless. He was a total bean counter in a dog-eat-dog corporation and highly competitive corporate world."

On June 23rd, the day after the Otter accident, Holland America Line stopped their 11-year business relationship with Wings of Alaska. All the other cruise lines had reinstated the company's onboard sales, but not Holland America Line. Kirk Lanterman decided it wasn't worth it to his company to take the risk of reinstating the Wings of Alaska tours.

On July 8th, John Litten picked up the telephone and dialed Holland America headquarters in Seattle. When he didn't reach Lanterman the first time, he called again.

"I'm sorry, John, but he's not taking any calls," said Dee Keegan, Lanterman's personal secretary.

"OK," John said. "You tell him I'm getting on a plane in Sitka on Monday morning and I'm coming down to Seattle to see him. Dee, you and I go way back to before Kirk Lanterman was in that job and I'm trusting that you can get me 15 minutes face-to-face with that guy."

"I can't say no to you, John, now can I? What should I tell him it's about?"

"Just tell him it's important enough for me to leave Sitka at the peak of the visitor season to talk to his funny-looking face for 15 minutes. And tell him I'm bringing a few friends."

Dee laughed heartily. "I'm on it, Mr. Litten."

John hung up the phone and started going through his Rolodex to find the phone number for some of the key tour operators that did business with Holland America. First on his call list was Bob Dindinger at Alaska Travel Adventures.

"Hi Bob, this is Litten. Clear your calendar for Monday because you're going with me to Seattle."

"What's this about, John?" Dindinger asked.

"That accident Wings had was a tragedy beyond words. But to a family like the Jacobsens that have such great hearts, it just doubles the size of that tragedy. I know we're all competitors for the same tourist business, but an accident can happen to any of us. If Wings can't get their tours back on the Holland ships it will really hurt them. I've got 15 minutes set up with Lanterman on Monday afternoon and I sure would like you to be there with me."

"Of course I'll be there," Bob Dindinger replied. "Who else is going?"

"I'm calling you, Bob Engelbrecht at TEMSCO and Bob Berto at Cruise Line Agency. I need some good soldiers along. Once all of you commit, I'll let Jacobsen know. It'll be the 'Bobs and John Show' and Lanterman won't have a chance."

"I don't know, John. Lanterman is a tough one. But I'm sure Jacobsen will appreciate your willingness to help."

"You know, Bob, it's not just Bob Jacobsen that this decision affects. The smartest thing Bob ever did was to have his sister Karen be the marketing person for them. She's the sweetest lady I've ever met in my whole life and she's done more to care for that company and that community than anyone I know. Not to mention the effect on all the Wings employees and the Ward family that bought the Taku Lodge. I think Lanterman's decision will have an impact on potentially any number of other tour operators."

"You're right about that, John," Bob Dindinger said. "I'll be there."

After hanging up and making a few more phone calls, John was successful in getting his dream team of soldiers together. By the time John Litten called to tell Bob Jacobsen to clear his schedule and make plans to meet him in Seattle on Monday, Bob didn't have a chance to say no, even though he tried. Litten's plan was in motion.

***

When "The Bobs" and John walked into Holland America headquarters on Monday afternoon they were immediately escorted to the company conference room overlooking downtown Seattle.

"Have a seat, gentlemen. I know why you're here," said Lanterman, who was already seated at the table waiting for them.

John and Bob Berto took seats next to Lanterman, while Bob Jacobsen and the others seated themselves across the conference table.

Always direct and to the point, Lanterman spoke first.

"Look, John, I'm hesitant to put the Wings' tours back on our ships. I'm worried about the liability to the company and I really don't want to look non-caring. Those people that died were passengers on a cruise," he said.

"Kirk, Wings is not just any company," John said. "You're already working with the best tour companies in Alaska and Wings is one of the best of the best in my opinion. They've had an impeccable safety record and have been industry leaders in promoting safety with other tour operators. For them to be cut off right now from selling on board your ships will completely ruin that company and that family. All the other cruise lines that temporarily suspended selling their tours inspected Wings and brought them back on board within a few days. Even World Explorer, whose passengers were the ones who died, brought them back to sell tours on board. You need to put them back on your ships."

"Do you all feel this strongly?" Lanterman asked the others assembled. "They're your competition. I'd think you wouldn't mind picking up some extra business."

"We all feel the same," Bob Berto said. "It was a tragic accident. If you put them back on, I'm sure they won't let you down."

"We may be competitors," Bob Engelbrecht said, "But we respect each other and Jacobsen would do the same if it was us."

Kirk Lanterman looked directly across the table at Bob Jacobsen, still not convinced.

"Can you guarantee me that this won't happen again, Bob?" Lanterman asked, leaning forward in his chair and taking a somewhat aggressive stance.

"I'm sorry, Mr. Lanterman, I can't guarantee we won't have another accident, just like you can't guarantee me that one of your captains won't mess up," Bob said, looking directly at him. "But I can guarantee I'll do everything possible - and then some - to avoid one."

Lanterman slowly leaned back in his chair and put both hands up behind his head. He hesitated for a moment. No one spoke.

"Well, I'll need to check with my insurance company, but assuming they agree, I'll give the go-ahead. Thanks for coming down, gentlemen."

"Thank you, Kirk," John said. "I told these guys there's a good heart down in there somewhere."

"Don't let that out of this room," Lanterman said.

Bob Dindinger wasn't sure, but as they walked out of the conference room an hour after the meeting began, he thought he saw Kirk Lanterman smile.

As John and "the Bobs" walked out of Lanterman's inner sanctum and through the offices of Holland America, there were a lot of inquisitive looks wondering how these young Alaska businessmen received an hour of their boss's time.

Immediately after the meeting, "the Bobs" and John headed back to SeaTac Airport. They had businesses to run and this was at the busiest time of the Alaska visitor season. Jacobsen was aware of just how big of a sacrifice of time and expense it had been for them all to come to Seattle to help Wings of Alaska on such short notice.

"Bobby, I'm pretty sure you'll be hearing from Holland America tomorrow that you're back on the ships," Litten said.

"What can I say except 'Thank you, guys,'" Bob said, swallowing hard.

"You might just let all of us beat you at golf a time or two," Bob Engelbrecht added.

"Hey, we can do that anyway," Bob Berto said. "How about you buy all of us dinner and drinks at our next Alaska Visitors Association meeting."

"Can do," Bob replied. "I can't believe I'm saying this, but I'll actually look forward to it."

Chapter Twenty-Six

You Should Take This Call

Josh Warner, like many attracted to life on the Last Frontier, was always something of an enigma. He lived aboard an old, dilapidated boat in Juneau's downtown Harris Harbor that he was perennially fixing up. Though obviously intelligent, he seemed to always be living on the fringes. In the summer of 1994, Josh was self-employed as the owner of a small printing and copying business. He was dating the daughter of one of the FAA officials investigating the Wings of Alaska accident, James McCoy. During the last week in July, Josh was a guest in the McCoy home.

Early in the morning Josh was in the living room when he heard James and his wife Sherrie talking quietly in the kitchen. After James left for work, Josh came into the kitchen for a cup of coffee. It was clear Sherrie wanted to talk.

"Good morning, Sherrie," Josh said.

"Oh, good morning. I didn't hear you get up. Any chance you overheard what Jim and I were talking about."

"I could tell you were having a private conversation so I just hung out in the living room. I couldn't hear what was being said, just that you two were talking. Is everything alright?" Josh asked.

"Well, honestly, I'm not supposed to even know about this, but you know that Wings of Alaska airplane accident that happened? Well, Jim is investigating it and he just told me that he's going to pull their certificate and that company is going to be out of business," she said. "Well, maybe they won't be out of business, but there sure as hell is going to be new owners."

"Why?" Josh asked.

"Jim says the FAA thinks they make their pilots fly in bad weather and he told me he is going to get them."

Since both Josh and Sherrie had work to go to, not much more was said on the subject at the time. Josh didn't give it much more thought until he saw Jim and Sherrie again later that night after Jim came home from work quite upset. Once again Jim was talking about the accident investigation when Josh entered the room. Jim looked up and immediately stopped talking.

"I'm sorry, Jim," Sherrie said. "I kind of told Josh a little bit about what was going on this morning."

"Oh well," Jim said. "I'm pretty pissed off right now, Josh," he said. "I had contacted a former employee of the company that said over the phone they had been expected to fly in bad weather, with equipment that wasn't certified for instruments, and then was made to fly in instrument conditions. On the phone, I understood the guy to say he was told he'd be fired if he complained about the weather. But when the guy sent in his written statement it was different and he didn't say any of that."

"So, I think the guy was coerced into changing his statement. I called the guy back today and I'm working on him, damn it."

Jim grabbed a bottle from the refrigerator. As he opened it, he proceeded to laugh. "So, I told the guy there could be problems with his pilot certification if he doesn't change his statement and tell me the truth."

"What do you mean?" Josh asked, a bit uneasy.

"Well, I get to give him check rides every so often. I ride in the plane with him and sign him off most every year for his commercial license renewal. I told him that this could have an effect on his paperwork and could adversely affect his certification. That ought to get him thinking. I told that guy I could make more trouble for him than that asshole at Wings of Alaska."

"Anyway, I'm trying to work around this pilot problem and I'm pretty sure it will happen. This company needs to be made an example of! That guy who runs Wings really pissed me off. He's a shrewd bastard who acts like he's a lawyer – probably because he's spent a lot of time in a courtroom, that prick."

Josh listened, but an uneasy feeling continued to grow with every new piece of information Jim shared.

"We're having trouble proving it because the pilots won't tell the truth – even the pilots that no longer work there - but it's just a matter of time before their certificate is pulled. If it's the last thing I do, I'm going to get them. Our investigator Kolvig thinks that prick

Jacobsen got all the pilots together in a room the night of the accident and concocted a story."

"I don't know, Jim," Josh said. "I know somebody who works for Wings and they're really happy working there." Josh could tell his reply made Jim more upset.

"I'm telling you this guy is a criminal and I'm going to get him. We're going to get their certificate pulled if it's the last thing we do."

"Ok, fellas," Sherri said. "Let's move this conversation onto something more positive. Anyway, I have a fabulous dinner tonight and we should get out and get the grill going. It's a beautiful night and we may not be having too much more of this great weather."

***

A few days later, Josh still couldn't get the conversation with the McCoys out of his mind. As Josh was getting fuel for his boat later that afternoon, he happened to run into John Jacobsen at the Aurora fuel dock in the harbor.

"I don't know anything about airplanes or airlines," Josh thought, "but I need to say or do something." At that moment Josh decided he'd share with John what he'd heard. He started up a conversation and it wasn't long before Josh was sharing all the details of his conversations with the McCoys.

"Josh, it would be great if you could give my brother Bob a call at the office and share what you just told me with him, too," John said, knowing how important it would be for Bob to hear a first-hand account of what FAA Inspector McCoy and his wife Sherrie had said to Josh.

"Yah, sure. I will call him from the pay phone when I get my boat back to my dock," Josh said. He finished fueling and the two men said goodbye.

"The hell with it," Josh thought to himself. "Jim McCoy would sure be pissed if he found out, but if it's one thing that really gets me, it's when people in authority abuse their power."

Chapter Twenty-Seven

"We're Going to Make an Example of Them"

Tim Miller would prove to be a hero to Bob and to the Wings of Alaska pilots for many reasons. Not only did he rearrange his schedule and fly to Juneau in the immediate aftermath of the accident, he became both a trusted advisor and a good friend.

Tim was a private pilot himself and he loved the Alaskan wilderness. He brought his two daughters to Alaska for fishing, camping and extended river-rafting trips on some of Alaska's wild and scenic rivers. Tim had worked with other aviation companies throughout Alaska prior to his work with Wings of Alaska. His experience proved invaluable to Bob, the pilots and to Wings' ability to navigate the legal issues facing the company after their first and only accident with fatalities.

From the first day Tim arrived in Juneau, people contacted by the FAA for questioning called Wings to relate the substance of the FAA's questioning of them. Tim also personally interviewed and took statements from current and former Wings pilots, as well as pilots and owners of other air-carriers around Southeast Alaska, many of whom had called Wings to relay their concerns over how the FAA was conducting its investigation.

Dave Brown of Alaska Coastal Airlines and Mike Salazar of Ketchikan Air Service, both told Tim what FAA inspectors had said to them. "We're going to make an example of Wings," and "The FAA is out to revoke their certificate," were the common themes shared. Both Brown and Salazar, as well as Jerry Scudero with Taquan Air, feared reprisals if either Kolvig or McCoy learned they had spoken with Tim Miller about their concerns.

Tim responded vigorously to the FAA's requests for information and documents and spent countless hours interviewing passengers on the four planes that returned safely to Juneau. He shared Bob's concern that FAA inspectors Bob Kolvig and Jim McCoy were biased and convinced that the pilots weren't telling the truth and had deliberately ignored FAA regulations. Within weeks of the accident, the FAA notified the company and the pilots involved in the rescue that enforcement action against them was underway. Tim was convinced the FAA's position wasn't substantiated by any of the evidence or interviews he conducted.

In early September, Tim sat down with one of the partners in his law firm, Jonathan Hoffman, to update him and outline his concerns about the FAA's investigation so far.

"I've completed telephone interviews with 30 of the 40 passengers on the four planes that returned to Juneau," Tim said. "Only three were somewhat concerned about the weather and all of them thought that their pilots did an excellent job. Overall, the passengers' recollections and observations support exactly what the pilots wrote in their statements to the NTSB. My investigation didn't reveal any problems with Wings' management or any evidence that the company encouraged or condoned pilots flying below FAA minimums. On the contrary, Wings management let a well-liked and respected tenured pilot go for violating company procedures about three weeks prior to the accident. My findings indicate they don't just talk safety, they expect it and enforce it."

"Well, that's all good," Mr. Hoffman replied, "but what about the one pilot statement the FAA is relying on to say he was pushed to fly in bad weather?"

"Well, that's interesting," Tim said. "That former pilot told the FAA he left the company on his own accord because he was pressured to fly in bad weather. That's just not true; Wings let him go. The truth is he flew for the company for just one summer season about three seasons earlier and was not invited back for the following season because of complaints about him from female staff. I was informed, and am attempting to verify, that he was also fired from his subsequent job due to allegations he made improper sexual advances."

"Well, I sure wouldn't want to use a guy like that as my star witness," Mr. Hoffman said.

"Not only didn't we find anything to back up that former employee's claims, but my investigation indicates intimidation on the part of the FAA's investigators to influence witness statements. I also believe the FAA investigators are conducting their investigation in violation of the FAA's own written enforcement policies. In that regard, I intend to depose both Kolvig and McCoy. I scheduled a meeting with the FAA Regional Manager in Anchorage to go over my concerns that the chief investigator seemed intent on manufacturing a case to revoke Wings' certificate, which would be an extremely rare response by the agency to one fatal accident."

"What was the Regional Manager's response to your meeting?" Mr. Hoffman asked.

"Well, he was receptive. He assigned another investigator from Anchorage to work with the Juneau investigators and our discussion ended with his assurances that Wings' operational authority, their certificate, would not be suspended or revoked. I think he also may have put another, more experienced attorney in charge of their side of the case."

"Well, it sounds like you're doing everything you can at this point."

"I hope so," Tim said. "The accident pilot George Coulter has already accepted a revocation of his commercial certificate and a six-month suspension of his private license as part of the FAA's enforcement action against him. His conduct that night can't be excused, but it certainly wasn't the kind of deliberate violation that the FAA inspector is attempting to establish against the other pilots and the company," Tim said.

"Unfortunately," he continued, "they're still going after the other four pilots for penalties and certificate actions." Mike Olsen, Kevin Kramer, James Roe, and Rusty Shaub all received official notices from the FAA of proposed suspension of their commercial pilot certificates. Tim was in the process of appealing those notices on their behalf.

"The FAA counsel and the Regional Director agreed to share the results of their investigation with us before any further decisions are made on enforcement actions against Wings or the other pilots and they promised to give us time to respond," Tim continued.

"I know Bob wants to defend his pilots," Tim said, "so depending on what the FAA does, we'll need to be ready for an NTBS hearing to prove the pilots' innocence. I'll need to take formal depositions from a lot of folks."

"Thanks for the update, Tim. Would you mind drafting up a letter so we can let the BAIG in London and their attorney, Ms. Marlowe, know where we stand on all this?" The BAIG, British Aviation Insurance Group, was the insurance underwriter for Wings' claims.

"No problem," Tim said. "I'll get on that right away. "It doesn't make sense to me that the FAA is going after Wings and hasn't even tried to sit down with company management team to talk about an evaluation of the accident and what Wings and the FAA local office have done to prevent a future occurrence, other than firing George."

"I agree," Mr. Hoffman said. "These accidents are so horrible for the victims, the survivors, the employees and the company."

Tim picked up his papers and prepared to leave the meeting. He was reinforced in the knowledge that he was doing everything he could to help Wings and the pilots caught in the FAA's crosshairs be able to stay in business. "I really like those guys at Wings," he said. "I can't find anything to indicate the other pilots were doing anything to warrant FAA sanctions and there's nothing I can find that even remotely indicates they aren't telling the truth about setting up to land on the river."

"Thanks, Tim," Mr. Hoffman said. "And thanks for keeping me posted on how this is going."

Chapter Twenty-Eight

Settlement Talks

Elizabeth Marlowe, a private attorney in San Francisco, was assigned by the British Aviation Insurance Group to defend Wings of Alaska in any tort litigation brought against the company.

Ms. Marlowe, as she liked to be called, grew up outside of the United States. In 1994, she was a 30-something, up-and-coming defense attorney for the BAIG. Rumor had it that she had a boyfriend in England who had a prominent position with the BAIG whom she was always trying to impress. Because Ms. Marlowe didn't have privileges to practice law in Alaska, the BAIG hired local attorney Deborah Holbrook, who had her own law practice in Juneau, to work as co-counsel with Ms. Marlowe.

On the evening of Ms. Marlowe's first visit to Juneau, a Jacobsen friend and attorney Jim Bradley arranged to have an informal dinner party at his home overlooking Gastineau Channel and Juneau's downtown harbors to welcome her and provide a chance for her to get to know Bob and Darlene and Deborah Holbrook. As soon as she walked through the door in her designer business suit, expensive jewelry and haughty attitude, Bob sensed possible trouble. Alaskans aren't generally impressed with people who are full-of-themselves, and it was obvious to him that Ms. Marlowe expected people to be quite impressed.

As she sat at dinner and recited her resume and experience, letting Deborah Holbrook and Jim Bradley know that she was clearly to be in charge of the entire legal affairs surrounding any tort claims and enforcement proceedings, Bob could already tell Ms. Marlowe's approach was not going to be particularly collaborative.

As was often the case, Bob's initial impressions turned out to be correct. Regarding Ms. Marlowe, however, interactions between Tim Miller, Deborah Holbrook, Bob and the accident victims families over the next two years, repeatedly illustrated Ms. Marlowe's outsized ego and combative approach were not in line with the interests of those she was hired to represent.

***

Larry Gard, Wanda Gard's son, was among the first of the survivors' families to have a run in with the legal process that resulted from the accident. He had come to Juneau from Savannah to take his mother home to Michigan just days before she was released from the hospital. Larry was shocked when his mother received a phone call the night before she was to fly home from a man who identified himself as representing Wings of Alaska's insurance company, the British Aviation Insurance Group.

"She probably lost a camera and we know she lost some glasses and a pen. If you could write down all those things she lost, we'd like to come over to the hotel tonight and settle up," the man said.

Larry was taken aback. "My mother is still physically recovering and she just lost her best friend. That's ridiculous," Larry said. What kind of person tries to pull that on a grieving older woman after this kind of tragedy," he thought to himself. "If this is the kind of people we are dealing with, these Wings people must be pretty awful."

"I can see you aren't ready to deal with this," the man said, quickly ending the conversation. "We will be in touch."

Wanda and Larry Gard departed Juneau the next day. A few weeks later a woman he came to know as Elizabeth Marlow arranged to come to Michigan to discuss a settlement with Wanda. They arranged to meet at a hotel conference room, where Ms. Marlow showed Wanda the back of a ticket. She alleged the ticket Wanda had purchased for the Wings flight clearly stated the maximum amount that could be paid for damages was $7,500. Although Wanda was initially ready to accept the offer and what she was being told by the "nice lady," Larry intervened on his mother's behalf.

"Clearly that amount doesn't apply in this case," Larry said. "My mother has no intention of being enriched by her trauma in the river or by Kathy's death, but I expect her to be treated fairly," he said.

By then, Larry had been able to have a better understanding of the financial loss to his mother from Kathy's death. Wanda and Kathy were roommates and had just begun construction on a new house on land they had purchased together. Larry knew Kathleen expected to work for least another 15 years and Wanda was counting on Kathleen's income to help pay their living expenses.

Larry later described his subsequent conversations with Ms. Marlow as "getting pretty ugly at times." On more than one occasion she ended their talks by hanging up on him. It took more than a year of back-and-forth heated conversations before Larry hired an attorney to represent his mother. Shortly thereafter, they reached a fair settlement.

***

Bob was frustrated that the settlement talks between Elizabeth Marlowe and the attorney for Alan and John Garner were also moving at a snail's pace. Though Bob didn't know much about Caroline Garner, he had spoken with her sons on a few occasions to help facilitate the return of her remains. He knew Caroline was a widow and Ms. Marlowe had told Bob that her family had connections to a ball-bearings company. Her sons were quiet, respectful and friendly and seemed appreciative of Wings' efforts.

In February 1995, Bob asked Ms. Marlowe why the Garner settlement was dragging on so long. The answer was clear: Alan and John Garner's attorney was non-responsive. Ms. Marlowe sent Bob seven months of communications she had sent to the Garner's attorney, with no response. Bob asked if he could contact the Garners directly, without going through their attorney, and she agreed.

By law, an attorney can't contact a person directly if legal counsel represents him or her, but for some reason that afternoon, Bob's frustration with the lack of progress in the settlement process and his concerns over the FAA investigation reached a boiling point. He decided it was time to call Alan Garner himself.

"Good afternoon, Alan," Bob said, after placing a call to Alan Garner's office. "I hope you and your brother are well."

"It's been difficult, but we're doing much better now. Thank you for asking."

"I'm really glad to hear that, Alan. I've said it to you both many times before. I want to express again how sorry we all are for the loss of your mother."

"We appreciate that, Bob, and everything your company did after our mother's death to find her and send her body home for burial. We know she would have wanted to be buried in Michigan," Alan said.

"We're grateful that could happen," Bob said. The two men paused for a moment and then Bob continued.

"I hope you don't mind that I'm contacting you directly. The attorney assigned to us from our insurance company, Ms. Marlowe, appears to be having difficulty getting ahold of your attorney Mr. Sloan to settle your claim."

"Honestly, Bob, we've had a really hard time getting ahold of our attorney as well," Alan said. "I'm not surprised he hasn't gotten back to her because he doesn't call us back either."

"I'm not exactly sure how this process works," Bob continued, "but I'd like to send you seven months of communication attempts from our attorney to yours. He just won't respond. If you and your brother are comfortable enough, you might consider finding a different attorney or reaching an agreement on your own and keeping the normal 33-percent contingent attorney fee. If you decide to let Mr. Sloan go, feel free to call me any time and you might consider settling directly with our attorney. It's my understanding that you have the right and opportunity to do that."

"My brother and I know this tragedy will never be behind us, but it sounds like we all want to complete this legal process and be able to move on from it," Alan said. "I'll talk to my brother and see if he wants to consider other ways to finalize a settlement."

"Thank you, Alan. Do feel free to contact our attorney Ms. Marlowe directly, if that's what you decide to do. Her office number is on the copies of the letters I'm going to FAX over to you right after we get off the phone, so you can see all of the correspondence that has been sent regarding your claim," Bob said. "I really want to reach a fair settlement with you and your brother. If there is anything I can do for you both, please call."

"Thank you, Bob," Alan replied. "We'll be in touch."

By late March of 1995, the Garner brothers were working directly with Ms. Marlowe and a settlement for their loss was reached soon after.

***

By the time Ms. Marlowe sat down for a meeting with the Schrantz family in March of 1996 to settle their tort claims, Dennis Schrantz absolutely and completely despised her.

Dennis Schrantz and his brothers were already waiting in the mediation conference room when Ms. Marlowe arrived. That day, she came in especially dressed to impress. Her crisp blue, designer business suit had clearly been tailored. Her perfect hair and makeup looked like she had hired a Hollywood makeup artist. Her high heels clicked on the floor as she entered the room and sat her briefcase on the conference table. The scent of her perfume filled the room. Ms. Marlowe always made an entrance.

The Schrantz family's attorney had informed them that Ms. Marlowe's position was that because their father Donald had a run in with skin cancer prior to his trip to Alaska and had a medical problem with his thyroid, his life was somehow worth less.

Dennis knew how vital and active his father had been. As a consultant himself, Dennis had never been one to be intimidated by reading piles of paperwork. He had read every legal document and letter between their family attorney and Ms. Marlowe. Though the Schrantz family found the thought of putting a value on the lives of their parents particularly difficult, Dennis found Ms. Marlowe's attempt to bring up bogus medical issues in her legal briefs and her last-minute efforts to dismiss their family's claims due to statute-of-limitations issues with their filing of the case, to be even more distasteful.

The attorneys had arranged for Retired Judge Justin Ripley to serve as an arbiter/mediator for the settlement talks. He was a distinguished older man with gray hair and a reputation for fairness.

"Good morning, boys," Ms. Marlowe said as she began her opening statement. "I just want you to know how sympathetic I am for your loss. I lost my dear granny recently and I know what it's like to lose people you love. I know exactly how you feel."

They weren't even three minutes into the settlement meeting when Elizabeth Marlowe's phony sympathy was all it took to set off Dennis Schrantz. He slapped his hands on the table, disturbing the big pile of legal papers in front of him.

"Don't stand there and act like you give a shit about us," Dennis said. "If you do, why did you file this brief just days ago to dismiss our case based on this bogus legal crap you pulled out of nowhere? You don't have a clue what it's like. Did you lose both of your parents in an airplane crash? This meeting is over."

Dennis picked up his papers and began to leave the room when Judge Ripley asked him to please listen for just a moment.

"Mr. Schrantz, I know this is extremely difficult. May I offer an office to you, your brothers and your attorney to use to talk privately? It takes a bit of work to schedule these meetings between everyone and I'm hoping that perhaps we can take a bit more advantage of our time here today?"

Dennis looked at his brothers, who nodded in agreement with the Judge. They all went out into the hall while their attorney spoke quietly with Judge Ripley to find out where he wanted them to go. It was obvious that if this meeting was going to go anywhere, Ms. Marlowe and the Schrantz' family needed to be in separate rooms.

"That woman is hateful," Dennis said to Joe. "She's a bold-faced liar."

Just then, the Schrantz attorney came out of the conference room to direct the brothers to a side office where Judge Ripley suggested they convene. From the corner of his eyes Dennis could see the judge talking to Elizabeth Marlowe. Judge Ripley didn't look too pleased.

Chapter Twenty-Nine

"I Think I Have to Quit"

It was a warm, sunny day at the end of July 1996, just over two years after the accident had occurred. Wings of Alaska's scheduled-airline business was back on track and the visitor operations had almost gotten to the 1993 levels. Bob continued to deal with the legal issues associated with the accident on almost a daily basis. While they had settled the other claims resulting from the tragedy by then, the claims for Rosa Maria Gomar de Vides and her family were still outstanding. He was preoccupied with preparing for the NTSB hearing regarding the FAA enforcement actions against his best pilots and Director of Operations, scheduled for a little more than two months away. Bob struggled with knowing that the FAA was determined to take away the four pilots' licenses and seriously impact their professional careers. The potential consequences to Wings were substantial and his frustrations and patience with the antics of Elizabeth Marlowe were getting out of hand.

Bob scheduled a conference call with Deborah Holbrook and Tim Miller to discuss what to do about the problems they were all having with Ms. Marlowe, especially her latest move to try to dismiss the claims of Rosa Maria Gomar de Vides and her family. From his last discussion with Deborah Holbrook, who he knew to be a cool and unflappable attorney, he could tell she too was reaching a breaking point in her relationship with Ms. Marlowe.

It was warm in his office, but as Deborah began to explain Ms. Marlowe's latest attempts to dismiss the claims, the rising redness on Bob's face wasn't from the outside temperature.

"Bob," Deborah began, "I know you already heard that Elizabeth pulled the settlement offer off the table that we had tentatively agreed to with Rosa's counsel. Not only did she make Rosa's attorneys look bad to their client, she absolutely pissed them off personally.

This could prove to be a very costly mistake for you, the BAIG and potentially for everyone."

"Deborah, I just don't think she's representing our interests," Bob said. "Isn't that her job, to represent us?"

"You're absolutely right," Tim Miller added. "She has a duty to you to keep you informed on what is going on with settlement discussions. Unfortunately for you, she's representing what she thinks are the BAIG's interests and I think she's trying to impress her boyfriend with how smart she is. In the end, she's going to cost the BAIG a lot more money to settle these claims."

"Go through it with me again, will you, Debbie," Bob asked.

"Basically, what she did was to keep postponing settling the claims and then when she finally pulled the offer off of the table, she said two things to opposing counsel. First, she claimed that the plaintiff had gone past the statute of limitations in bringing a legal claim forward. Second, she said that because of an obscure legal loophole she found, regarding conflict of laws between various countries, the plaintiffs were not entitled to anything for the loss of life."

Deborah continued. "The idea behind the conflict of laws - in a nutshell - is that since Rosa's family comes from Guatemala and bought their tour tickets for your flight on a foreign-built ship and in international waters, a conflict of laws exists between the international laws governing the ship and the civil laws of Alaska governing the tort claim. She basically said Rosa's family couldn't claim anything."

"That's ridiculous," Bob said. "Rosa lost her mother and her two children on our airplane and has experienced untold trauma. How can Marlowe even do that without my knowledge or my consent?"

"Well, Bob," Deborah said quietly, "I can't answer your question directly or comment on if she can win this legal argument in court, but I can tell you that I personally think it's unethical and I feel that if she continues down this path, I will have to quit. I don't want to be a party to the direction she's going."

Bob sat quietly for a moment, trying to digest everything he was hearing.

He could hear the planes taking off outside his hangar and he watched a small Cessna land on the Juneau airport runway.

"I understand, Debbie. And I want to ask you to please hang in there a little bit longer. At this point, even if I have to hire a personal attorney and bring suit against Marlowe and the BAIG for not representing Wings properly, I will not agree to this."

"Thank you, Bob," Deborah said. "I know you and I know your family. I also know how much you've done to try to do the right thing for everyone involved. Unfortunately, she's already pulled the offer and completely upset Rosa's attorney, Tim Cook. His firm, Speiser, Krause, Madole & Cook, is one of the biggest and most influential law firms in the country. Technically, I am co-counsel with Elizabeth and I work for the BAIG, so I'm not even sure I should be the one having this conversation with you, but I wanted you to completely understand what is going on. If these claims aren't settled and your FAA and NTSB issues aren't resolved in your favor, Rosa's excellent attorneys could go after everything you own in a much bigger way. There is the potential that they could seek punitive damages which your insurance company won't cover and take every asset Wings has – your airplanes, your hangar, your bank accounts - and there is a possibility of piercing the Wings' corporate veil and going after the personal assets of the owners – basically everyone in your family."

"Look, Bob. I don't think that's going to happen," Deborah said, sensing Bob's anxiety. "It's a worst-case scenario that I believe you needed to be made aware of."

"You don't need to worry about that now," Tim Miller added. "But we do need to come up with a strategy for getting Ms. Marlowe to back down from this crazy stuff and get back to representing your wishes and your interests." Tim stressed the words "Ms. Marlowe," giving a horrible impression of Marlowe's accent in the process.

"That's an understatement," Bob said, taking a sip of water. "Any ideas?"

"I think we need to make sure the BAIG in London is clear about what's going on. I'm not sure they completely know what our Elizabeth has been up to or the consequences that could result from her actions," Tim said.

"I agree," Deborah added. "You may also want to make sure Allen Shattuck is in the loop. He's your insurance agent and the BAIG is his underwriter for other policies as well, so he has a relationship with those folks that's separate from our Ms. Marlowe."

"Maybe we need to start calling her Cruella de Vil," Tim said, trying to lift the mood.

"OK, then," Deborah added with a laugh. "I have no comment on that, but I will hang in there for a little longer while you try to work this out, Bob. Let me know when things change or how I can help."

"Please Debbie, just don't quit," Bob said. "Thanks for the call today. I'll be in touch."

As soon as the group ended the conference call, Bob dialed Tim Miller back.

"Tim," Bob said. "What do you think about me bringing my friend Jim Bradley into this? He's a great man and a great attorney and I think Debbie has worked with him in the past. If I have to bring legal action against Marlowe and the BAIG, I think it might be a good idea to loop Mr. Bradley in now."

"That's a good idea, Bob," Tim replied. "But I also like the idea of having Shattuck send a letter up-the-food-chain in the BAIG to see if they can get you someone else to represent you or if they can move Marlowe along toward a settlement."

"I agree," Bob said. "But we need to move quickly. The NTSB hearing for our pilots is nine weeks out. Hey what's one more legal action when we're having this much fun already," he said sarcastically. "Where are we with the NTSB and the FAA enforcement actions?"

"We're getting ready for trial," Tim said. "I've interviewed 36 of 40 passengers. The remaining four won't call me back. I'm planning to come to Juneau in two weeks so we'll have lots of time to go over everything."

"Ok, thanks, Tim. I'll buy you dinner when you come up."

"I don't know, Bob. After what you've been going through lately, I think I'll need to buy you dinner accompanied with some 17-year-old Scotch and we'll let the BAIG pay for it."

"Works for me," Bob said. Bob reached for the water glass on his desk. "That sounds like what we need to do and I look forward to your visit in two weeks. Thanks, Tim. See you soon."

Pilot Kevin Kramer, Tammy Kramer, Pilot Mike Olsen, Sarah Olsen and Pilot Rusty Shaub at the Governor's House receiving Heroism Awards.

Gov. Walter J. Hickel, Pilot Rusty Shaub and his wife Thyes Shaub.

Chapter Thirty

Three Miracles

For the next two years Rosa's life primarily consisted of doing every kind of healing or therapy suggested to her. Counseling, exercise, bodywork, Chinese medicine, Hindu medicine, the Pranic Healing method, prayer and meditation – she used them all.

And she cried. She cried a lot.

Rosa would wake every morning thinking the horrors had all been a bad dream. And then she would walk into the empty bedrooms of Maria and Miguel only to be catapulted back to her new reality. Day after lonely day, Rosa would face anew that the emptiness she felt wasn't a dream at all.

And she cried.

"What am I to do with all this pain?" she asked herself again and again. "How do other mothers who lost their children survive? Is there a way out?"

There were mornings when Rosa was sure there was no way out of her pain, in spite of her determined efforts to find relief. Days, months, and years passed. The pain remained.

"How is it that those lawyers can put a value on the lives that have been lost?" she asked her attorneys one morning as the settlement talks dragged on. Rosa's brother handled most of what needed to be done on the legal front with her attorneys and he tried not to drag her into the details of their work unless they absolutely had to, knowing how each call seemed to push her back into her despair.

Despite it all, Rosa was determined not to give up her quest to find a measure of healing. She found a teacher who was able to help her learn to release and balance her energy. She found classes that helped her get in touch with her spirit. She traveled to the Unites States to visit the healing center founded by noted psychiatrist and author on the five stages of grief and death and dying, Elisabeth Kübler-Ross. She found answers there and she found a measure of comfort sharing her experience with others who also experienced great loss. Through her relentless pursuit of recovery and through learning techniques through Pranic Healing, meditation and yoga, Rosa found relief from some of her pain.

She came to a faith so deep and so profound she was able to let go and find a measure of light again. In her desire to help herself and help others, Rosa experienced a miracle. She found the reason she believed God had kept her here on earth.

The miracle had a name: Lucia.

"Rosa Maria," a friend called to say one day almost three years after the accident. "There's a newborn baby from a tribe outside the city who desperately needs a home. Would you consider taking her for the night?"

Rosa was shocked, but she knew from her own tragedy and the spiritual healing work she had been practicing, that she had to respond to the plea for help.

"Of course," Rosa said. "How can I help? Where do I go and what do I need to do?"

A few hours later Rosa was holding a beautiful one-day old infant girl in her arms. That night, Lucia slept in Rosa's bed. The next morning, when Rosa woke, she was overcome with anxiety. She realized she didn't have anything for a newborn – no clothes, not enough formula, no diapers or blankets. She needed to shop for everything a baby needed if she was to help this child.

When the beautiful baby girl awoke, she was smiling. At that moment, Rosa realized that her life was no longer about her and no longer about her grief. She realized that after three years of grieving, this baby – who she would ultimately adopt and raise as her own – had needs that were more important than hers. Lucia was first and Rosa was second. In Lucia's smile, Rosa found her purpose.

Eighteen months later, Rosa adopted another baby girl, Ana. Four months after Ana arrived, Rosa received another call. "There's a boy, and he looks just like you. You have to come down and see him. He needs help."

"But I'm already so busy with a baby and an almost-two-year-old," Rosa said.

"But he looks just like you."

"How can I say no," Rosa said.

The moment she saw him, Rosa now had three miracles. And the miracles had names: Lucia, Ana and Jesus.

Chapter Thirty-One

Can I Sue My Lawyer?

Jim Bradley was a big man who commanded a big presence. He'd been a partner in the firm Robertson, Monagle, Eastaugh & Bradley, prior to leaving to form a practice with two other attorneys, Kathy Kolkhorst and Bill Ruddy, toward the later days of his successful career. Bob trusted that Jim would always have his best interests at heart. He had employed the services of his law firm at other times since forming Wings of Alaska and always had a good working relationship with Jim. Plus, he trusted Jim's common-sense approach and legal experience, which included having tried cases in front of the United States Supreme Court during his illustrious career.

After thinking about all the potential negative impacts Elizabeth Marlowe's approach could have on the pilots, his family and his business, Bob decided the money he would spend on additional legal counsel would be a small price for advice on how to proceed with Ms. Marlowe. He was determined to do whatever was in Rosa's interest and necessary to stop Ms. Marlowe's representation of his company. He decided to arrange a consultation at Jim's office two days after his phone call with Deborah Holbrook and Tim Miller.

The law firm of Bradley, Ruddy and Kolkhorst was on the second floor of one of Juneau's largest professional office buildings, the Jordan Creek Center, located not far from the Wings of Alaska hangar. When Bob came through the door, he was immediately greeted warmly by one of Jim's partners, Bill Ruddy, who was standing in the open reception area welcoming one of his own clients. Like Jim, Bill had a kind and friendly demeanor and was also a tough litigator. Bob had worked with Bill in the 1980s to settle a claim when a passenger had slipped and fallen on the Juneau Airport ramp after exiting a Wings of Alaska plane.

"Hey, Good morning, Bob. Good to see you again. How are you doing?"

"Doing, OK, Bill. How are you and Kathy and your kids?"

"We're all doing fine," Bill said. "Why don't you take a seat and I'm sure Jim will be right with you."

"Can I get you coffee or anything?" the office receptionist asked politely.

"No thank you, I'm good," Bob replied. As he was about to take a seat, Jim Bradley came out of his office, smiling broadly. Just seeing him made Bob feel better about the task at hand. Jim always helped to put everything into perspective.

"Come on into my private sanctum," Jim said. "I've been reading over what you sent me yesterday and this is all quite interesting."

"I'm not sure interesting is the word I'd use, Jim."

"No, I'm sure you have a few other choice words for this situation," Jim said. "But let's go over a few of the facts and see if we can come up with the right solution to help the folks in London see the light of day. By-the-way, what time is it over there now anyway?"

Bob took a seat across from Jim's desk. Jim walked over to his printer and grabbed two copies of what he'd been working on and handed one to Bob.

"From what I can see," Jim said, "you and your company have done a fantastic job of handling an incredibly tragic and difficult situation. The fact that you've settled all the tort claims so far with the exception of Rosa's and that the settled claims have been accommodated for just under $2.4 million is somewhat remarkable given the history of Alaska jury awards and settlements. I'm sure that has a lot to do with the relationships your team developed and the actions you all took with the individuals and families involved."

"Thank you for saying that, Jim. You're very kind."

"The hell I'm kind," Jim boomed. "It's the damn truth and the letter Shattuck sends to the BAIG needs to tell them that! They need to know you're respected throughout this region and the whole state, for God sakes! I'm sure your Wings' insurance account was sought after by lots of brokers and underwriters in Alaska. Allen needs to let those Brits know that too."

"Also, Bob, I think Allen needs to tell them you're not a loose cannon. I get the impression from talking with Tim Miller and Debbie Holbrook that Ms. Marlowe may have painted you to the BAIG as something other than the businessman you are."

Bob looked down at the paper Jim had given him with message points to suggest for Allen Shattuck to include in a letter to the British Aviation Insurance Group.

"I'm not sure how she's painted me, Jim, but I'm pretty sure how she's painted herself. She thinks she is smarter than Tim Miller, Debbie Holbrook, Bart Rozell, Tim Cook –

Rosa's attorneys - and everyone else involved in this situation. She is pretty sure I'm a small-town boy who never left home and is lucky to have her on my team."

"Well, it's clear to me, Bob, that she's not playing on anybody's team but her own. You and I know baseball and we know how a good team works and she's not on anybody's team. If she were representing you and the BAIG, she would have settled Rosa's claim for the $1.5 million that was previously on the table. That's a reasonable amount considering what Rosa went through with the loss of her mother and two children."

Bob looked up from the paper and looked directly at Jim. "Thanks again for saying that, Jim. I agree with you that she isn't representing anything close to what is just or what we want," Bob said. "You know how I feel about Rosa. She's an incredible human being and I couldn't feel worse about what happened to her, her entire family and all the victims. And to have Ms. Marlowe play her hard-ball legal games with Rosa and other victims' counsel without even consulting me, it's stupid, it's unethical and it really pisses me off. Rosa's claims should have been settled a long time ago."

Bob's voice shook. He used the back of his sleeve to wipe away the tears he felt slowly moving down his cheek.

Jim handed Bob a Kleenex and pretended to look for something in the files on his desk. After a minute of fumbling with his files, he brought the conversation back to the business at hand.

"So, from what I can see, the time to settle this final claim is now. It's absolutely unconscionable that in a case like this Ms. Marlowe hasn't spoken with you directly for roughly one year. Is that correct?"

"Yes, Jim, that's correct. The last time we spoke was in August last year when she thought the Gomar de Vides claim could be settled for somewhere between our $1.5 million offer and $2 million. I believe she had authority from the BAIG to go up to $2 million. Sometime after that she pulled our $1.5 million offer off the table and came up with that questionable statute of limitations clause and the conflict of laws issue."

Jim shook his head and rolled his eyes. "That legal move has the potential to be an expensive error," he said. "Shattuck needs to tell the Brits in addition to offending the plaintiff's counsel and making them look bad, it is folly to put all the legal eggs in one basket like that. It's asinine and it's not good legal strategy. Tim Cook's law firm will decimate her."

"Well, like I said, she thinks she's smarter than everyone," Bob said. "Depositions of our Wings' pilots, including Coulter, in preparation for the NTSB hearing are scheduled for the week of August 19 at the Baranof Hotel. That's just two weeks away. It's my understanding that Rosa, or someone representing her from the Speiser Krause law firm, is coming to Juneau to attend those depositions. On top of that, she pissed off George Coulter and his attorney and they've become uncooperative. It's not a good situation."

Jim stood up from his desk and slowly walked to the window. He stood there for a moment before turning back toward Bob, with a concerned look on his face. The light behind him that was coming through the window silhouetted his large frame, however, Bob could clearly make out the concern on his face.

"Bob, Tim Miller told me that all the attorneys had agreed on a mediator for the settlement talks and the mediator's time was reserved. Is that right?"

"Yes, that's my understanding from Debbie Holbrook," Bob said. "The mediator was scheduled and now Marlowe wants the mediator cancelled. Using her conflict of laws and statute of limitations arguments, she's saying that the BAIG doesn't owe Rosa anything."

"Well, I think all the sane people think a mediator is a good idea. Allen needs to tell the BAIG that."

"I take it you are you agreeing with me that Ms. Marlowe isn't representing our interests as you would? Tim Miller wants to call her Cruella de Vil. He's pretty sure she kills puppies in her time off."

Jim laughed heartily. "That's not really funny, though," he said. "It might be true. She gives us lawyers a bad name."

Jim sat back down at his desk. "If I understand correctly, you've already had two delays with the NTSB law judge, which has given you ample opportunity to settle the claims. I understand the hearing in front of Administrative Law Judge Mullins is scheduled for the first week of October and a third delay is extremely unlikely."

"That's right," Bob said. "Howard Martin, the FAA lawyer going after our pilots and our Director of Operations, told Tim Miller there would be no further extensions. Our pilots and our company will face the judge in just two months and my pilots want to prove their innocence from the FAA allegations. Tim Miller has done a great job deposing the FAA investigators and getting them to admit they didn't provide exculpatory evidence in their report to the FAA legal department. But honestly, no one knows what will happen when we go into that hearing with Judge Mullins. It's a crapshoot, Jim. Our guys are really tired of having this FAA-imposed stress hanging over their heads and their careers. And I can't even imagine the stress this is causing for Rosa."

"Well, I think Allen should stress that in his letter too. If Marlowe can't settle this before the hearing..." Jim's voice trailed off. "Let me just say, it's in the BAIG's best interest and everyone's best interest to get this thing settled."

Bob and Jim agreed that Jim would send another copy of the message points they had developed to Allen Shattuck via FAX and that Bob would meet with Allen to help draft a final letter to the BAIG.

"Thanks for meeting with me today, Jim," Bob said. "I've never had to sue a lawyer before. I sure hope we don't have to now, but if I do, we are quite fortunate to have you on our side."

"Well, I think Allen will do a great job letting the BAIG know what's been going on. I'm confident that Ms. Marlowe's bosses are the only ones who can tell Cruella to quit messing with us puppies! I'm also confident we can get this all back on track. Bob, and we'll get this legal stuff in line."

Chapter Thirty-Two

A Photographic Memory and a Louisiana Drawl

Howard Martin was a private pilot and an experienced FAA lawyer. Although he wasn't the original attorney assigned to the Wings of Alaska investigation, Bob and Tim Miller's objections to the handling of the investigation by Kolvig and McCoy had reached the ears of higher ups in the FAA organization. The FAA Division Manager in Anchorage, Dick Gordon, had decided to bring Howard Martin into the investigation.

"Howard, I need you to take a hard look at this investigative file and take the lead on it," Dick said. "I'm not looking to try to pin error, I want you to look at all the angles, all the evidence, and see where it falls out."

"I've looked at what the investigators sent up in their report," Howard said, "and it's pretty clear when it comes to the accident pilot, but it's a mixed bag when it comes to the other four pilots who were up the river that night."

"Look, Howard. I'm opening up the checkbook. Get on a plane, travel where you need to go, talk to the 40 other passengers who were on the four planes that landed safely. Look at all the evidence against the company and against the other pilots. Build the case you see. I trust you."

"Well, thanks, Dick," Howard replied slowly. "We've got the pilots' statements to the NTSB that they descended below 500 feet to land on the river, but we will need to get a lot more information from the other passengers to build a case."

"Well from what I heard through the grapevine, Bob Kolvig told an operator in Southeast that the FAA brought in another attorney who is a fat fuck with a photographic memory, so I'm putting this case in your big fat hands." Dick Gordon smiled.

"Well, I like the photographic memory part," Howard said in his thickest Louisiana drawl. "That's true, Sir. But I can't believe anybody would call this 'ol Cajun boy a fat fuck!"

"Well don't quote me on that," Dick said. "I'm just passing on a rumor I heard."

"You're going to need to have a talk with your boys in Southeast at FSDO 5," Howard said.

Dick Gordon's look turned serious. "Let's just say they've been spoken to," he said.

***

Both Howard Martin and Tim Miller were getting ready to go to trial at the NTSB hearing and face the judge. As is common practice, attorneys take depositions from witnesses and exchange general information pertinent to their positions in both letters and through conversations.

Both attorneys were talking to each other in general terms about their evidence and planning for trial. Two NTSB administrative hearings for the pilots to prove their innocence had been postponed. Howard Martin stressed to Tim Miller that there would not be a third delay.

"Based on passenger observations, but most remarkably by the express admissions of the pilots interviewed, the agency will show in three of these cases that the pilots descended below 500 feet," Howard Martin said to Tim Miller during a call about the case. "In as much as there were no landings executed in any of these cases, the issue for the judge is whether there was a present intent to land when your clients breached the altitude restrictions or whether they were simply setting up to land if the weather deterioration mandated it."

"Well, Howard, I think you know what our position is on that. The other pilots had no motivation in talking to the NTSB or the FAA to do anything but tell the truth. I don't understand what you have to base anything on that they're lying to you. Floatplane pilots all over the world, and especially in Southeast Alaska, use landing on the water as a safe alternative when they encounter marginal weather. If that is contrary to the rule, show it to me in the Federal Aviation Regulations."

"Our evidence may be circumstantial, Tim, but we think we can prove that the guys were intentionally trying to get under the weather to have better visibility. We believe they were scud running just like the accident pilot Coulter was. I'm sure the administrative judge is going to want to know why every pilot descended below 500 feet before visibility improved."

"That's not correct, Howard, and you can't prove that." Tim replied. "They descended below 500 feet to land and the third pilot, Roe, never descended to land at all."

Tim Miller listened intently as Howard continued to set out the basis for the FAA's actions. When Howard was finished, he paused a moment before he spoke.

"Well, thank you for your time and for your letter outlining your case, Howard. You witnessed and have copies of the depositions we took from Kolvig and McCoy. I think it's pretty clear that the original investigation and the report they sent you clearly left out exculpatory evidence. In addition to omitting beneficial evidence to Shaub and the company, you learned of the bias Kolvig and McCoy exhibited while building their investigative file."

By law, police and other criminal investigators, such as the FBI, are supposed to share evidence that can exonerate or is favorable to a person being investigated. Tim had Kolvig and McCoy clearly admitting in their depositions that they had left letters out of their investigative file from a long list of pilots saying no one in Wings management ever pressured them to fly in bad weather or condoned flying below FAA minimums. The letters they received that were not included in the investigative file all said Wings management, and especially Shaub, never pressured pilots to fly.

"I'm not basing our case on their investigative file alone, Tim, but I can see where you could think they might be going too hard on the company and the other pilots besides George Coulter and that could get Judge Mullins attention and not look good for our side."

"You think so?" Tim said, a bit sarcastically. "There's absolutely no evidence that Wings management or Rusty Shaub ever pressured pilots to fly in bad weather and Kolvig and McCoy's depositions clearly show they formed their biased opinions early on in the investigation, well before they ever sat down with a single one of the pilots."

"Look, Tim," Howard replied. "I know neither of us want to take this to a hearing if we can come up with a way around that."

"It's been more than two years, Howard, and you're aware of how the pilots and Wings responded after the accident. The pilots and the company went over and above what was expected in every instance. Hell, the guys you're going after put their lives on the line to go back and find survivors and recover the victims when the United States Coast Guard walked away. All the pilots and employees at Wings have been living with an incredible amount of stress over your ability to pull their certificates and put them out of business. Let me talk to them and let's see if we can keep a conversation going between us to see if we can find another way."

"I think we're open to that, Tim. I'll have some conversations on my end as well."

The attorneys said goodbye and Tim Miller sat quietly at his desk staring out of the window.

"I'm sure I can win this case," Tim thought, "but I have to advise Bob and the pilots it might be best to see if we can negotiate a small civil penalty that could be removed from their records after a period of time. They deserve their day in court, but if I could get the FAA to back off the suspensions of the pilots' licenses and end this thing with a censure, it might be best for everyone. It's their call, though."

Tim's administrative assistant Althea Tisk came into his office as he was writing notes to himself after his conversation with Howard Martin.

"Your wife and daughters are here to take you to lunch," Althea said.

Tim looked up and smiled at Althea. "I'm always ready for a lunch date with the three most beautiful ladies in my life."

Chapter Thirty-Three

An End and A Beginning

Bob sat quietly in the small conference room at the Wings hangar, not entirely sure where to begin. He knew George Coulter didn't understand why Wings could no longer employ him after the accident. Not too long after the FAA had revoked George's pilot credentials, George came to Bob to ask if he could use one of the Wings' airplanes to do some flying required to get his pilot's license back. George was angry and hurt that Bob had said no.

Bob had helped George find other work after Wings had let him go and the company continued to take care of George's attorney fees throughout his own dealings with the FAA. Bob understood George's anger and frustration with him. Their friendship and business relationship pre-dated Wings of Alaska. Bob had been advised, and knew in his heart, that he couldn't put the company in any more jeopardy by allowing George to use Wings' planes. He knew George was suffering and couldn't comprehend the actions Wings took in the aftermath of the accident.

Each of the other four pilots who the FAA was going after had their own difficult decisions to make. Bob was concerned how they would feel if he recommended they accept a slap on the wrist compared to the six month suspension of flying that Tim Miller and Howard Martin were discussing as a way to avoid going to a trial. He wanted to be careful to not influence them one way or another, even though he personally thought that by reaching a settlement with Howard and the FAA would allow all to put the accident behind them and make a fresh start. As Bob sat in the conference room getting ready to speak to each of the pilots individually, he weighed his words carefully.

"Morning, Mike," he said, as Mike Olsen entered. "How's it going?"

"Oh, you know. About the same," Mike replied.

"Well, Mike, as I mentioned earlier, Tim Miller and I wanted to talk with you about a decision that only you can make. Tim is on the speaker phone so you can ask him any questions directly and if at any time you would like to talk to Tim privately, I will leave the room. No problem?"

"No problem with me," Mike said.

"That's great," Bob said, "so let's lay out what's in front of us."

"Sounds good to me," Mike said.

Bob thought Mike looked thinner than usual. He knew how the past two years had taken its toll on this man who Bob considered to be one of the best, natural pilots in Alaska. He flashed on a memory of the pained expression on Mike's face in a photograph taken when Alaska's Governor Walter Hickel had given Mike, Rusty, and Kevin a state medal for heroism for having rescued the survivors after the crash. He knew Mike didn't consider himself a hero. He also knew the added weight the FAA investigation was forcing Mike to carry.

"Well, Mike," Bob continued. "As you know, Tim has been preparing to present our case to NTSB Law Judge Mullins early next month. Tim and the FAA's attorney have been talking about a settlement to avoid the NTSB proceedings and both have agreed that if you want to settle, the FAA is willing to go from their original enforcement action of suspending your license for six months to no suspension. It would be a $1000 fine, which Wings would pay on your behalf. It's my understanding that the civil penalty sanction would be removed from your record after a period of time."

"Does this mean I'm admitting I did something wrong?" Mike asked.

"Look Mike," Tim said. "I think I can win this at the hearing. The FAA's case is built on the statements you all gave to the NTSB saying you went below 500 feet with the intention to land. That's why they dropped their enforcement action against Jim Roe – because he never said in his NTSB statement that he flew below 500 feet or set up to land. The rest of their case is simply based on circumstantial evidence and it's weak. The problem is, that once we go face the NTSB law judge, we have no control over what happens. If, by some chance, we don't win, the potential cost to each of you as pilots will be much greater."

"I'm pissed that the FAA has put you into this position at all," Bob said. "But it's where we are and it's your decision as to what you want to do."

"I'm pissed off too, because I know the truth about what happened. I know we told everyone the truth. None of us busted any FAA regulations except Coulter," Mike said, "but I'm enough of a realist to know that the truth doesn't always matter."

The group sat quietly.

"Bob, let me talk this over with my wife Sarah and let you know," Mike said. "I realize I have to make a decision in the next few weeks before the hearing is scheduled, but I want to know what my family and the other pilots think. To be honest though, I'd really just like this all to be over. I think the other guys probably feel the same way, though we haven't talked about it. This is our careers, our reputations, and our future livelihoods we're talking about."

"I agree with you Mike, the FAA has been completely unjust and out-of-control all along. We all know you're an amazing pilot and an amazing person, and none of us deserve what they're putting us through," Bob said.

Mike looked directly at Bob then slowly stood up. He was a man of few words and he had already said more about how he was feeling than Bob had heard him say for months. "Thanks," he said. "Do you want me to get Rusty?"

"That would be great," Bob said, walking over to put his hand on Mike's shoulder. "I'll see you Monday. Try to have a good weekend."

"I'll try," Mike said. "You too."

Bob grabbed a bottle of water from the small refrigerator in the room and sat back down. "Are you still there, Tim?" he asked.

"Yep, I'm still on the phone. We're going to have to stop meeting like this," he quipped. "I'm spending more time talking with you than I am with my wife and daughters."

"Can you send a bill to the FAA for that?" Bob asked.

Just then Rusty entered the room. The conversation with Mike was about to repeat two more times.

Ultimately, after more than two years of the FAA trying to suspend their pilots' licenses, Kevin Kramer, Mike Olsen and Rusty Shaub reluctantly agreed to accept the FAA's settlement offer. They chose to accept a small fine, rather than pit their careers and future livelihoods against the power and money of the federal government. The years of stress from the FAA had taken its toll.

Kathleen Pruneski and Wanda Gard in Alaska. (Courtesy of Wanda Gard)

Wanda Gard and former Wings of Alaska Pilot Mike Olsen when Wanda returned to the site of the accident in 1997. (From "Alaska Heroes: A Call to Courage")

Chapter Thirty-Four

Coming Back, Healing and Forgiveness

Mike Olsen had been a pilot throughout Alaska for more than 17 years when he pulled Wanda Gard from the Taku River. Wanda had been going in and out of consciousness for at least 15 of the last 45 minutes she had been in the water and was hypothermic when she was rescued. When Mike hooked an oar into Wanda's life vest and pulled her toward the floats of his plane, he knew she was close to death. Her weight, coupled with the weight of the glacial silt saturated into her clothing, made it impossible for Mike alone to pull her onto the float and into the plane.

In her conscious moments, Wanda could hear Mike encouraging her. "Hold on," he kept repeating, as he pulled her as close to the airplane float as he could. "You're going to make it, Ma'am. Hold on. Help is coming."

When help did come, it arrived in the form of Ken Ward, Paul Scriber and Ted Zurdowski from their skiff on the river. They helped Mike lift Wanda into the plane through the rear door of the Otter. Mike had already demonstrated his incredible skill as a pilot landing his plane through the fog 10 minutes earlier using Rusty's plane as a reference point. Now, his personal courage and commitment to doing what was right came together to guide him through the zero visibility fog and make it safely back to the waiting ambulances in Juneau.

When Mike stopped in to see Wanda at Bartlett Hospital after the accident, she already knew she loved him. When Wanda decided to return to Juneau to visit the scene of her partner and best friend's death years later, the love between her and the man she called her personal angel deepened.

Carl Ramseth was working in the Wings office when a call came in from Wanda asking if it would be possible for her to visit the site of the accident. Carl knew Mike had been the pilot who rescued Wanda and he also knew Mike had a riverboat with jet propulsion that would be the perfect way to take her to the accident site. When he was asked, Mike didn't hesitate to help.

"I can't believe we lucked out to have such a beautiful day," Mike said, as he piloted his boat up the river. Before setting out, Mike introduced Wanda to his wife Sarah and two children, Riley and Abby. Wanda was grateful to have a chance to make the connection with Mike's family. And she was especially grateful to be able to go to the last spot where she and Kathleen Pruneski had been alive together on this earth.

"Kathleen loved Alaska so much," Wanda said. "She never got to travel much when she was younger and she had such a wonderful sense of adventure."

Wanda wondered aloud how things might have been different if Kathleen hadn't switched seats with Rosa to take the co-pilot's seat on the trip back from the lodge. "It's strange how life is," Wanda said. "I've come to terms with God's will, but it doesn't make me miss her any less."

"I'm sure that's true," Mike said. "Life ain't easy and there's a whole lot we just can't understand."

Mike reminded Wanda of the actor Sam Elliot; he looked like him – including sporting a broad, beautiful mustache - and he sounded like him too. There was something about the way Mike sounded when he agreed with her that day that made Wanda feel like everything really would be OK. She was so grateful he was with her on the river. She was happy she would be able to remember not just fear, cold and fog and her near-death experience when she thought of that river, but she'd be able to remember the incredible beauty of Alaska. She was happy she would remember the kindness Mike shared.

"If you ever come to Michigan, you'll have to come to visit," Wanda said.

From that day forward, every Christmas Mike's children received presents in the mail from Wanda. And Wanda regularly kept in touch with Kieran O'Farrell as well, even attending her wedding ceremony aboard a boat years after the accident.

When Mike decided the time had come to retire from flying and take a less stressful job with an oil pipeline company, he was coincidentally transferred to Marshall, Michigan, Wanda's hometown. It gave him the opportunity to visit. On one of his visits to her apartment Mike was shocked by another incredible gift Wanda decided to give his children.

"Now you don't say anything, Mike. Don't say one word. I've got something I need you to know, so you just listen," Wanda began. "You know I don't have a lot, but I want you to know that I put your children, Abby and Riley, in my will to receive part of my estate when I pass away. You gave me all these extra years of life. I know you never expected anything, but this is my way of saying thank you for what you did for me and to thank you for being the man you are."

Mike looked up at Wanda. Usually a man of few words, as he gulped back his tears, there was nothing he could say.

***

Florence Schrantz always had a deep spiritual connection to her ancestors. When she would take her children to the cemetery, she would talk to the graves of those who had passed. Dennis Schrantz grew up believing that life doesn't end when someone leaves this world.

Despite his belief, however, Dennis was overwhelmed by the grief he felt at the loss of both his mother and father and a pervasive sadness dominated his life for years after the accident. He often found himself staring at a photo of his mother that was taken at the Taku Lodge just before her death. His parents' camera had been retrieved from the airplane and returned to them by the Alaska State Troopers. The Schrantz family was amazed they were able to develop the film. One of the pictures showed Florence standing on the lawn at Taku Glacier Lodge in front of the Hole-in-the-Wall Glacier, smiling and waving.

It always seemed to Dennis when he looked at that photo that his mother was waving good-bye.

As a consultant on prison systems, Dennis' work brought him to Alaska in 2015 and he decided to visit Juneau. He promised his wife Nicki that he wouldn't take a plane or a boat out to the crash site, but he knew he wanted to meet Bob and then hike out as far as he could along Gastineau Channel toward the confluence of the Taku River.

While standing on Juneau's downtown dock the morning he arrived, Dennis suddenly felt a horrible chill come over his entire body. Stunned and immobile for a moment, he said out loud to no one in particular, "This is where Dad died."

Like so many people's spiritual experiences that science can't explain, Dennis was standing on the exact spot where his father had been transferred into a waiting ambulance after Rusty brought him back to Juneau. He felt as if he could hear his mother's voice talking to his father, telling him to hurry up and come with her, as she wouldn't have wanted to go on to the next world without him.

Later that morning, Dennis had breakfast with Bob at a coffee shop at the Baranof Hotel. Bob invited Rusty to join them. As the three men sat having their coffee, Dennis listened to Rusty and Bob recount the details of the accident and the rescue. Rusty shared his belief that the cruise ship doctor's decision to move Donald in his hypothermic state contributed to his heart attack and eventual death. Dennis hadn't known all the details of that part of the story. He thought about the cold that had come over him earlier that morning as Rusty confirmed it was indeed the last spot where his father was alive and where he had been put into the waiting ambulances.

Rusty held back tears as he recounted pulling Donald from the water. Bob wiped away a tear as they talked about the accident's aftermath. When the three men finished their meeting, Dennis hugged Rusty and Bob and thanked them for what they had done.

"You know, Bob," Dennis said. "All of our family has the highest regard for you. I hope you know we don't blame you for what happened. My parents always taught us that the Lord doesn't give you a stone that you can't carry. I believe these things are part of how we gain grace. It's been a gift to me to be able to be here today. I never realized the burden that you guys have carried and I'm honored to be able to support you to let go of that stone."

It was still relatively warm and sunny in Juneau and after saying goodbye, Dennis decided to drive his rental car south along Thane Road. He had been told that when he reached the end of the road, he would find a trailhead that led to a beach. From there, Dennis decided to hike along the shoreline to where he could get a good view of where the Channel and the Taku River meet.

"I guess I just want to get as close to where the plane went down as I can," he thought. In his backpack, Dennis had brought along a Buddhist prayer book, a book on Alaska by James Michner, and a photo of his parents. He planned to find a place where he could read, pray and meditate. The Michner book he was reading had a section that described the life of salmon that end up in the Taku River.

As he sat along the water's edge, Dennis felt he could almost see the spot where his parent's plane had gone down.

After a few wonderful hours praying, meditating, reading the Michner book out loud on the beach, and taking the time to thank his parents for all they did for their family, Dennis heard the rushing waters of the tide coming back into the channel. He grabbed up his things and realized the water had almost surrounded the spot where he had been sitting. He was slipping and sliding on the rocks as he walked through the now knee-deep water to make it back to higher ground. He could feel his parents' presence.

Dennis Schrantz didn't consider himself to be a religious man, but in that moment he felt a deep and spiritual connection to his parents and understood why his mother had always talked to her ancestors.

Chapter Thirty-Five

June 20, 2014

"It was June 20, 2014, exactly twenty years after the accident. The Jacobsen family decided to host a party to welcome Rosa Maria back to Juneau. Past and present Wings of Alaska pilots and other employees, their husbands, wives, children and guests filled the Jacobsens' kitchen, living and dining rooms and spilled out onto the home's front deck. Bob was outside on the next-door neighbor's front lawn manning a grill and Darlene was busy serving their guests.

It was Karen Jacobsen who welcomed the guests-of-honor when they arrived at her brother's front door. She welcomed them with her usual warmth, humor and enthusiasm. Karen ushered the Gomar de Vides family into the kitchen, quickly making introductions all around.

Rosa Maria and her family were clearly overwhelmed, but soon warmed to the assembled crowd. Rosa proudly introduced her teen-aged children, citing each of their talents and accomplishments. Bob and Darlene stopped what they had been doing and personally greeted and extended their hospitality to each of the new guests, making sure their plates and glasses were soon filled with food and drink.

One-by-one people in the crowd introduced themselves to Rosa and told her the role they had played in the tragedy exactly 20 years before.

"Yes, I think I remember you," Rosa said when Rusty Shaub introduced himself.

Both Susan Christianson and former Wings pilot Joe Sprague just happened to be in Juneau the night of the barbecue. They were delighted to be invited to attend. Joe Sprague had worked for the company in the late 1980s and early 1990s and Susan had first met Bob in 1996 when they worked together on a community project. They had both spoken with Bob many times about the 1994 accident and its aftermath. Susan was glad Bob asked her to bring her camera to document the event and from behind the anonymity of its lens, she watched as Rosa and her family laughed and spread joy, love and healing to everyone they spoke to throughout the evening.

While Rosa made it a point to speak with everyone gathered, she spent the most time talking with Thyes Shaub, Rusty's wife. The two women were wrapped in conversation on the deck while Jesus played the Jacobsens' piano in the living room and Ana, Lucia and her cousin Gonzalo admired the scenic view. Rosa was genuinely interested in listening to Thyes talk about the effects the accident had had on the rescue pilots, Wings employees and the Juneau community.

"Rusty and one of the other pilots who rescued the survivors, Mike Olsen, quit flying not too long after the accident," Thyes said. "They took it really hard."

"I can't believe how selfish I've been," Rosa said, after quietly listening to Thyes. "I never thought about your grief or the effect on any of you, only my own."

"You and the word 'selfish' don't go together at all," Thyes replied. "You're such an inspiration. The children you've adopted are so beautiful and it's amazing to see and hear what you have done with your life. I'm so honored to meet you. We are all so happy you came back."

Bob gently interrupted the conversation to talk with Rosa about the things she and her family wanted to do while in Juneau. He knew the children wanted to see whales and he had arranged to take her family and a few friends on a whale-watching excursion the next day, courtesy of Bob Janes and Dawn Wolf with Gastineau Guiding. Bob and Rosa spoke briefly about visiting the Catholic Shrine of St. Therese and having dinner together the next evening. He knew Rosa's main goal was to travel to the Taku River on a boat to hold a family memorial at the crash site. Bob assured her that he would make all the necessary arrangements.

Bob Jacobsen with Rosa's cousin Gonzolo and her three adopted children Ana, Lucia and Jesus visiting Alaska in 2014.

Rosa Maria Gomar de Vides with Karen Jacobsen on June 22, 2014 at the Jacobsen's gathering.

Chapter Thirty-Six

Roses on the River

It was yet another beautiful sunny day in Juneau; the kind of day Juneau residents dream about in the darkness of winter. The temperature was in the 70s and there was a slight breeze in the air. You could see the snow on the top of the mountain peaks, set against the trees.

The gathering at Bob and Darlene's house, the loving conversations Rosa had with past and current Wings employees, and the fun whale watching adventure and Shrine of St. Therese visit with Rosa and her children, all contributed to the incredible healing taking place in Bob's heart.

As Bob and Darlene loaded up the family's Bayliner with food and supplies for their trip on the Taku River with Rosa and her family, Bob took special care to set aside the beautiful flowers he and his sister Karen had cut from her rose garden just hours before. He wasn't sure how he would feel taking Rosa to the spot where the plane had gone down, where she had lost Maria and Miguel and her mother Rosita, but he knew it wasn't his feelings that mattered. Rosa had come a long way, physically, emotionally and spiritually, to make her way back to Juneau. The day was about Rosa and he wanted to do everything possible to make it a perfect day.

"It must have taken a lot of courage for you to decide to come back," Bob heard Darlene say when Rosa and the children and her cousin were settled on the boat.

"There are things in my life that get me stuck, that I want to change," Rosa said. "I had such a fear of coming. After talking on the phone with my counselor David and Bob, the fear disappeared. I had no more excuses for being stuck. I knew I had to go forward. It was like a big portal I had to step through. That's why I came."

"I am so happy I came," Rosa said. "The first day was such a surprise to me. We went to the dock where the Wings planes take off. When I heard the planes accelerate to leave, it was such a happy moment hearing them. I loved that moment and that was surprising for me."

"Then when I went to this dinner at your house, Darlene. There were all these pilots and all these people who came. There were so many people who suffered my pain for all these years and I realized I had been so selfish, never thinking of all the consequences this created in all these people," Rosa said.

"You, Rosa, have been such an amazing example to everyone," Darlene said. "You are not now and have never been selfish. You were so loving and kind to all the pilots and everyone was so happy to meet your new family."

Rosa, Lucia, Ana, Jesus and Gonzolo scurried around checking out the boat as Bob untied the lines that had been securing it to the dock.

When they reached the spot on the river where the plane had gone down, Bob turned off the engine and Rosa asked everyone for silence. Bob took out the flowers they had cut from Karen's garden.

Rosa and the children took out flowers they had also brought aboard. Rosa opened an envelope with photos of Maria, Miguel and Rosa Maria. They all prayed, cried softly, and sat silently, each lost in their own thoughts and feelings. Rosa sat for a long time with her eyes closed in quiet meditation and contemplation.

Slowly she got up, followed by her cousin, her children, Bob and Darlene. One-by-one they tossed the flowers into the river. Rosa held the photos on her heart before gently letting them go into the water.

The sun sparkled on the river's surface. The water was calm and as smooth as a mirror. The trees on the shore seemed to reach out to them as if to say, "Well done." The boat was barely moving on the water.

Rosa looked out over the Taku River. The boat was encircled in flowers and rose petals. She reached into her bag and took out some of the healing herbs she had brought from Guatemala, she said another prayer and then threw the herbs into the water to join the swirling flower petals.

Sunbeams streamed down through the high clouds. Light reflected off the flower petals.

"I came to Alaska to truly let go, to find what forgiveness feels like, to leave the fear in the past and to give thanks to God for making me the woman I am today," Rosa said. "Something I am taking home with me is the power and the capacity to live life the best

I can, taking in as much guidance as I can get. I want to be open to all beings of love and light. I am taking this with me and I am so blessed. I really am so happy I came."

Suddenly, as if on Divine cue, a single seal popped up playfully amidst the roses on the river, reminding Rosa of the beauty of life that still surrounded her. She felt at peace.

Rosa Maria Gomar de Vides in 2014 on the Taku River.

Epilogue

by Bob Jacobsen

I will forever carry the weight of this accident on my shoulders and the pain and suffering it caused for so many people. It is my hope that by sharing the tragic details of the absolute worst failure that ever happened in my life and for my company, lessons will be learned.

There are still far too many aviation accidents happening 30 years later. If telling this story can help prevent one accident, prevent one fatality or save one child's unnecessary death, it will be worth it. I know we can do better. Any profit or royalties that may come my way from this book will be invested in aviation safety.

When I look back at what could have been different, there are things we could have improved upon, not the least of which is communication. We understand how important communication, respect and teamwork are, yet in our case, the lack of each turned out to be the root cause of a fatal accident. If I had a do-over, I would have been more forthcoming with my friend George Coulter – the person who taught me to fly – about growth and changes in our organization and his role in it. I shouldn't have let friendship and loyalty to George get in my way of the decisions that needed to be made.

I am proud of the way our team dealt with the immediate aftermath. I can never properly thank Mike Olsen, Rusty Shaub and Kevin Kramer for their courageous efforts rescuing victims the night of the accident. They risked their lives to save others. All three pilots have suffered post-traumatic stress and I should never have allowed a meeting with the FAA without an attorney present. I never would have if there was a clue that instead of seeing our rescue pilots as heroes who risked their lives to save others, Kolvig, McCoy and the FAA would go after their licenses and their careers. The extra pain Rusty, Mike and Kevin endured as a result of working for Wings of Alaska is on me. Unfortunately for us, Rusty resigned as our Director of Operations as soon as our legal battles ended and Mike Olsen ended his accomplished aviation career about the same time. I shoulder responsibility for how my decisions contributed to their plight and the accident's cause.

Words can never express my sincere appreciation to Ken Ward, Bob Engelbrecht, Mike Stedman, Paul Scriber, Ted Zurdowski, Jim and John Jacobsen, Carl Ramseth, Matt Roys, Don Bach, Errol Champion, Bill Corbus, Mitch Falk, Scotty McAllister, Wayne Alex, Pete Lind, Dick Callahan and others who helped recover our victims when the United States Coast Guard and Alaska State Troopers left the scene. Not only were these men impacted by their heroic contributions; their wives, partners and families were as well and they deserve my over-due gratitude.

Allen Shattuck, Tim Miller, Deborah Holbrook and Jim Bradley were experts in their fields who believed in Wings and that the FAA's desire to destroy our pilots and shut Wings down was inappropriate and unjust. Even the plaintiff's counsel for our survivors and victims' families, gentlemen like Tim Cook and Bart Rozell, and eventually FAA attorney Howard Martin, were fair minded and had "what's the right thing to do" at the center of their concern. Our world could use more fair-minded adversaries like Bart, Tim and Howard these days. And the British Aviation Insurance Group led by Ross Marlin, Steve Lake and eventually Elizabeth Marlow, ultimately were fair in their treatment of claims for all the survivors and the families of victims.

And there were other standouts as well. Joe Sprague, who came forward to help us during our dispute with the FAA, men like Kirk Thomas, Dave Brown, Mike Salazar, Jerry Scudero, whistleblower Josh Warner, and others, who spoke out against what the FAA inspectors were saying and doing.

I learned the value of standing up to bullies and governmental authority if necessary. While the NTSB and FAA inspectors had a job to do, some went well beyond their authority by leaving out exculpatory evidence that didn't fit their working theory of what occurred. When their beliefs weren't supported by a preponderance of evidence, they left that information out of their reports. How often do we see this abuse of governmental authority by rogue federal, state, or local justice officers who represent the power of government? It's difficult to be on the receiving end of that abuse. Standing up for our pilots and our company the best I could, I learned the value of fighting for truth and justice.

I learned the importance of kindness and following your heart. Thirty years later I have the letters and cards sent in support during our difficult time. The words said then still touch my heart and inspire me to be kinder to others.

I learned the value of community. Growing up in Juneau, Alaska, was a blessing. A sense of community still exists. Like many other true communities, we have our divides, yet when someone is in need we come together. We know as Alaskans that our environment is bigger and stronger than we are and to survive we help each other. That value built our community, our state and our nation. I hope it's a value our family can pass on to the next generation of Alaskans.

From Rosa Maria Gomar de Vides, from Margarette de Munoz, from Wanda Gard, the Schrantz family, the Garner family and from visiting the past for this book, I learned that healing is possible. In remembering and writing about our tragedy, I have shed tears, yet somehow, through becoming vulnerable to everything I pushed aside, I learned a new strategy. I witnessed firsthand how people turned their personal tragedies into triumphs.

Friends, colleagues and business partners ask what we might accomplish in telling this story. Some express fears that our successor business, 30 accident-free years later, might be negatively impacted with the telling of this story. We are still part of a great aviation company serving visitors from all over the world showing them receding glaciers and taking them to the 100-year-old, historic Taku Glacier Lodge. It's the best tour in Alaska rated as such by visitors for years. I understand my partners' concerns, yet our successor company has learned from the mistakes we made and the details of our tragic event will forever reinforce their commitment to safety.

My goal for this project is that it will inspire other owners of airline companies, their managers, and pilots who haven't experienced a fatal loss to look inward and expand their perspective on managing and mitigating risk. Our industry continues to have too many accidents where someone's ego blurs good judgment and injuries or deaths result. The death of John Kennedy, Jr., near Martha's Vineyard, the loss of Alaska's great Senator Ted Stevens near Dillingham, Alaska, the deaths of four generations of Hansen family men in Chamberlain, South Dakota, the loss of Kobe Bryant, his daughter and seven others, and the six fatalities in Murrietta, California in 2023, are all examples of poor judgment costing lives. We keep making the same mistakes. We can't wait for the government or regulatory authorities to make aviation safer. It's up to us. We can do a better job of stopping these senseless and preventable accidents.

Acknowledgments and Participants

In addition to the individuals and organizations listed below who were involved in or impacted by the Wings of Alaska accident, many people helped to bring this book into reality. To those who read drafts, provided critiques, and especially to those who gave of their time to be interviewed or share their story, you have our deepest gratitude. If the sharing of this story helps prevent future accidents or provides hope or healing to anyone who suffered a tragedy of their own, it will be because of your encouragement and participation. The author and the Jacobsen family are forever grateful.

To follow is a list of the individuals and organizations named in the book that played an important part in this story.

1. **Alex, Wayne** – A lifelong Alaska logger, fisherman and skipper of the *Pacific Bell* who was hired to help recover the aircraft.

2. **Bach, Don** – Leader of the Wings maintenance program. He helped recover victims and the aircraft.

3. **Bartlett Memorial Hospital** – Local Juneau hospital whose physicians and nurses treated survivors and provided exceptional care to victims and their families.

4. **Berto, Bob** – Visitor industry leader based in Ketchikan, Alaska, who supported Wings of Alaska.

5. **Bittick, Sgt. Robert** – A member of the Alaska State Troopers who interviewed survivors and family members after the accident.

6. **Bradley, Jim** – Long-time, well-respected Juneau attorney who provided guidance for the varied legal issues that arose.

7. **Brown, Dave** – A local pilot and owner of his own air-taxi company who flew the Taku River corridor the night of the accident and provided a statement to the FAA and to Tim Miller.

8. **Callahan, Dick** – Juneau commercial diver hired to assist with the recovery of the aircraft.

9. **Champion, Errol** – Longtime Juneau resident in the logging and aviation business who provided support and assistance to find the downed aircraft.

10. **Childres, Gary** – Federal Aviation Administration inspector out of the Anchorage, Alaska office, assigned to assist with the accident investigation.

11. **Christianson, Susan** – Author, neighbor of George and Karen Coulter, and friend.

12. **Cogan, Stew** – A neighbor of Jim Jacobsen in Issaquah, Washington.

13. **Cook, Tim** – Attorney with Spieser, Krause, Madole and Cook Law Firm who represented Rosa and the Guatemalan victims.

14. **Corbus, Bill** – Owner of Alaska Electric Light & Power Company, who helped in the aircraft recovery effort.

15. **Coulter, George** – 12-year Wings of Alaska pilot who taught Bob Jacobsen and Drew Haag to fly in Eugene, Oregon.

16. **Coulter, Karen** – Wife of George Coulter.

17. **Crumbaker, Ron** – Manager, Juneau Flight Standards District Office.

18. **Day, Kirby** – Ship's agent for Southeast Stevedore, who became a Princess Cruise Line operations manager.

19. **de Munoz, Margarette** – One of the accident's surviving passengers from Guatemala.

20. **Dindinger, Bob** – Visitor-industry leader, based in Juneau, who helped support Wings.

21. **Emberton, Dick** – AEL&P employee at Annex Creek.

22. **Engelbrecht, Bob** – Visitor industry leader and manager of TEMSCO Helicopters, who supported Wings and assisted in the rescue operations.

23. **Falk, Mitch** – Owner of Gumption Freight Service providing barge service to remote communities throughout Southeast Alaska, who was hired to assist with the airplane recovery.

24. **Fenster, Mike** – Longtime Alaska pilot and previous manager and owner of Wings of Alaska.

25. **Fernandez, Leonel** – Brother-in-law of Rosa Maria Gomar de Vidas who came to Alaska after the accident.

26. **Fredricks, Dave** – Wings of Alaska pilot who helped locate the downed aircraft.

27. **Gard, Wanda** – A survivor of the accident from Marshall, Michigan.

28. **Garner, Alan** – Son of Caroline Garner, an accident victim.

29. **Garner, Caroline** – An accident victim from Michigan.

30. **Garner, John** – Son of Caroline Garner, an accident victim.

31. **Glen, Pat** – Former Executive VP and Chief Operating Officer at Alaska Airlines.

32. **Gomar de Fernandez, Haydee** – Sister of Rosa Maria Gomar de Vidas, who came to Juneau after the accident.

33. **Gomar de Vides, Rosa Maria** – Survivor of the accident from Guatemala.

34. **Gomar, Anna** – Adopted child of Rosa Maria Gomar de Vides.

35. **Gomar, Jesus** – Adopted child of Rosa Maria Gomar de Vides.

36. **Gomar, Lucia** – Adopted child of Rosa Maria Gomar de Vides.

37. **Gomar de Vides, Miguel "Miguelito"** – Five-year-old boy who survived the accident and later died in the Taku River and whose body was never found.

38. **Gomar de Vides, Maria** – Seven-year-old girl who survived the accident and later died in the Taku River.

39. **Gomar, Miguel Angel** – Brother of Rosa Maria Gomar de Vidas, who came to Juneau after the accident.

40. **Gomar, Rosita** – One of the accident victims, mother of Rosa Maria Gomar de Vidas and grandmother of Maria and Miguel.

41. **Gomar, Susie** – Sister-in-law of Rosa Maria Gomar de Vides, who came to Juneau after the accident.

42. **Gordon, Dick** – Manager of FAA Flight Standards District Office for Alaska, based in Anchorage.

43. **Gordon, Terry** – Assistant Manager of the FAA Flight Standards District Office in Juneau.

44. **Haag, Drew** – Cofounder of Wings of Alaska, pilot and former Alaska Airlines Captain.

45. **Hickel, Walter** – Former Alaska Governor who honored Wings of Alaska pilots with the Alaska Heroism Award.

46. **Hoffman, Jonathan** – Law partner in Portland-based firm Martin, Bishoff, Langslett and Hoffman, who represented Wings. (Now MB Law Group).

47. **Holbrook, Deborah** – Juneau-based attorney who represented Wings and was co-counsel with the BAIG's other attorney in the tort proceedings.

48. **Jacobsen, Jerry** – Matriarch of the Jacobsen family and former Wings of Alaska bookkeeper.

49. **Jacobsen, Jim** – An Alaska Airlines Captain and owner of Wings of Alaska who

assisted in the recovery efforts.

50. **Jacobsen, John** – An employee and owner of Wings of Alaska who assisted in the recovery efforts.

51. **Jacobsen, Karen** – An employee and owner of Wings of Alaska who spearheaded Wings coordination with victims' families.

52. **Jacobsen, Nathaniel** – Son of Bob and Darlene Jacobsen.

53. **Jacobsen, Christian** – Son of Bob and Darlene Jacobsen.

54. **Jacobsen, Darlene** – Wife of Bob Jacobsen and employee of Alaska Airlines.

55. **Janes, Bob and Dawn Wolf** – Owners of Gastineau Guiding, who provided a whale-watching excursion to Rosa's family on the 20th anniversary of the accident.

56. **Juneau Fire Department EMTs** – Responded to the accident in a variety of capacities and participated in grief counseling with Wings employees.

57. **Keegan, Dee** – Executive Secretary for Kirk Lanterman at Holland America Line.

58. **Kenny, Michael (Bishop)** – Bishop of the Catholic Church in Southeast Alaska.

59. **Kolvig, Bob** – FAA Principle Operations Inspector in the Juneau Flight Standards District Office who was responsible for oversight of Wings of Alaska and became lead investigator on the accident.

60. **Kramer, Kevin** – Pilot for Wings of Alaska who rescued Rosa Maria Gomar de Vides.

61. **Lake, Steven** – Senior Claims Adjuster for the British Aviation Insurance Group (BAIG).

62. **Lanterman, Kirk** – President, CEO of Holland America Line.

63. **Lind, Pete** – Commercial diver who was hired to assist with recovery efforts.

64. **Litten, John** – Visitor industry leader based in Sitka, Alaska, who came to Wings assistance.

65. **Lown, Robin** – Alaska State Trooper Lieutenant who interviewed survivors.

66. **Lucas, John** – Wings of Alaska owner and Chief Financial Officer.

67. **Luttman, Gretchen** – Friend of Rosa Maria Gomar de Vidas, who came to Juneau after the accident.

68. **Marland, Ross** – The British Aviation Insurance Group (BAIG) legal officer.

69. **Marlowe, Elizabeth** – Pseudonym for the attorney assigned by the BAIG insurance underwriter to represent Wings of Alaska in the tort claims.

70. **Martin, Howard** – FAA attorney in Anchorage, who prosecuted the enforcement actions against the Wings of Alaska pilots.

71. **McAllister, Scott** – Longtime fisherman and skipper of the *Owyhee,* who was hired to assist with the downed aircraft recovery efforts.

72. **McCoy, Jim** – FAA inspector in the Juneau Flight Standards District Office.

73. **McCoy, Sherrie** – Wife of Jim McCoy.

74. **Miller, Tim** – Attorney who was hired to defend Wings of Alaska's interests with respect to the FAA enforcement proceedings.

75. **Morin, Bill** – Helped establish the Crew Resource Management Education Program at Alaska Airlines.

76. **Mullins, Judge Roger** – NTSB Administrative Law Judge who would decide the FAA enforcement action.

77. **O'Farrell, Kieren** – Wings of Alaska pilot who befriended accident victim Wanda Gard.

78. **Olsen, Mike** – Wings of Alaska pilot who rescued Wanda Gard and George Coulter.

79. **Pratt, Bill** – Juneau professional counselor who assisted George Coulter and Wings of Alaska employees after the accident.

80. **Pruneski, Kathleen** – Accident victim from Marshall, Michigan.

81. **Ramseth, Carl** – Wings of Alaska employee and flight follower the night of the accident.

82. **Rinehart, Mike** – Chairman of the Crew Resource Management Education Program at Alaska Airlines.

83. **Rinkenberger, Scott** – Wings of Alaska manager in 2014.

84. **Ripley, Judge** – Arbiter/Mediator for the Schrantz brothers in Michigan.

85. **Roe, James** – Wings of Alaska pilot who flew one of the five Otters the night of the accident.

86. **Rozell, Bart** – Co-counsel plaintiff attorney to Tim Cook, representing Guatemalan victims in the tort claims.

87. **Roys, Matt** – A former Wings of Alaska employee who assisted in the aircraft recovery efforts.

88. **Roys, Sharol** – Wife of Matt Roys.

89. **Ruddy, Bill** – Juneau attorney and partner of Jim Bradley.

90. **Sagmoen, Terri** – Friend of Darlene Jacobsen.

91. **Salazar, Mike** – Pilot and owner of Ketchikan Air Service.

92. **Schrantz, Dennis** – Son of Donald and Florence Schrantz, accident victims, who visited Juneau in 2015.

93. **Schrantz, Donald** – Accident victim from New York.

94. **Schrantz, Florence** – Accident victim from New York.

95. **Schrantz, Joe** – Son of Donald and Florence Schrantz, accident victims.

96. **Schrantz, Timothy** – Son of Donald and Florence Schrantz, accident victims.

97. **Schrantz, Michael** – Son of Donald and Florence Schrantz, accident victims.

98. **Scriber, Paul** – Employee of the Taku Glacier Lodge, who helped rescue survivors the night of the accident.

99. **Scudero, Jerry** – Pilot and owner of Taquan Air Service in Ketchikan.

100. **Shattuck, Allen** – Owner/partner in Shattuck and Grummett Insurance Agency who helped in the recovery of the plane and victims.

101. **Shaub, Rusty** – Pilot and Wings of Alaska Director of Operations who rescued Margarette de Munoz and Donald Schrantz.

102. **Shaub, Thyes** – Wife of Rusty Shaub.

103. **Sprague, Joe** – Former Wings of Alaska pilot.

104. **Stedman, Mike** – Wings of Alaska Chief Pilot.

105. **Thomas, Kirk** – Pilot and former owner of Tyee Airlines in Ketchikan.

106. **Thomas, Mike** – Wings of Alaska maintenance technician who helped recover victims and the aircraft.

107. **Thomas, Ralph** – A reporter from the Anchorage Daily News.

108. **Tisk, Althea** – Executive Assistant to attorney Tim Miller.

109. **Valentine, Ron** – World Explorer Cruises executive in the San Francisco office.

110. **Van Campen, James** – Deckhand on the *Owyhee*

111. V**ecci, Ray** – Chief Operating Officer of Alaska Airlines

112. **Vides, Byron** – Husband of Rosa and father of victims Maria and Miguel.

113. **Ward, Ken** – Owner of the Taku Glacier Lodge who helped rescue survivors the night of the accident and who helped recover victims.

114. **Ward, Michelle** – Owner of the Taku Glacier Lodge and wife of Ken.

115. **Ward, Mike, Natalie and Buzz** – Children of Ken and Michelle Ward, who played with the Gomar de Vides children.

116. **Warner, Josh** – Whistle-blower regarding FAA investigation of Wings of Alaska.

117. **Wings of Alaska Employees and Families** – Every employee and their family members whose lives were affected by this accident.

118. **Zurdowski, Ted** – Employee of the Taku Glacier Lodge, who helped rescue survivors the night of the accident.

About the Author

About Susan Stark Christianson

Susan Stark Christianson is an award-winning author, film producer, former journalist, mother and grandmother. She has owned the advertising and public relations firm Christianson Communications in Juneau, Alaska, for more than 25 years. She served as a former Deputy Director of Communications for the State of Alaska, Office of the Governor, and worked as an award-winning journalist. Her first book, published in 2010, "Women's Voices: The Wisdom of the Grandmothers," grew from her involvement with the Women's Voices Project. In 2015 she produced the documentary "The Wisdom of the Grandmothers," which aired on 85 PBS and FNX stations to an audience of almost 89 million in more than 34.5 million households. In 2018, Susan was named a Rasmuson Foundation Fellowship Award recipient. Along with her work on "Flying With Wings," Susan is currently producing the documentary "Indigenous Prophecy Today."

About Bob Jacobsen

Bob Jacobsen is a lifelong Juneau resident. He received degrees in Public Administration and Political Science at the University of Oregon in 1977. With family and friends, he founded Wings of Alaska in 1982 and Wings Airways in 2002. He was selected Citizen of the Year by the Juneau Chamber of Commerce in 2005. Bob took an active role statewide in the visitor and aviation industries, serving as President of the Alaska Visitor Association and the Alaska Air Carriers Association. He was inducted into the Alaska Business Hall of Fame in 2006. Though he and his partners sold Wings of Alaska in 2008 to a Portland, Oregon company, Bob continues to be involved in Alaska aviation and tourism. He and his wife, Darlene, and their two sons continue to live in Juneau, Alaska. Both young men work in the Alaska aviation industry.

For more information or to order more copies please go to www.FlyingWithWings.com